Thanks for
supporting RVER!
Bill Carman

Copyright © 2018 Kentucky Wild, LLC

All rights reserved.

ISBN: 1986026736
ISBN-13: 978-1986026734

Cover Photo by Bill Carman (Kentucky Wild, LLC)

Cover Design by SavyPrint (www.savyprint.com)

ACKNOWLEDGEMENTS

Some of the stories in this book began over forty years ago, and therefore it is a challenge to acknowledge everyone who deserves thanks over such a span of time. Nevertheless, I'll give it a go. Thank you, Savanna Clark of SavyPrint, whose graphic design skills birthed this book.

A big shout-out to Jay Houston, author and elk hunting guru, who encouraged me to transform a folder crammed with stories into a book. Kudos to John Sanders and Randy Waterhouse, whose photography skills and good humor are evident in these pages. I truly appreciate the friendship of Tom VanArsdall who accompanied me on many of my adventures. Thank you Kim Delozier for helping me realize that maybe I have a few bears in my backseat that could be penned to paper.

I owe a debt of gratitude to Steve Rinella, with whom I have shared campfires and who continues to inspire me. Thanks to Don Thomas, author and Traditional Bowhunter Magazine editor, whose stories captivate me and whose editing made many of my stories magazine-worthy. I owe gratitude to my son Drew Carman and his wife Maria D'Amato Carman, for designing my website and Kentucky Wild logos, which are used as the icons for each chapter.

Also, a big thank you to my daughter, Sarah Behler, whose photographic and computer skills helped me turn my passion into a business. My son and fishing buddy, Dan Carman, is much appreciated for his companionship and for teaching his sons to fly fish. Thanks to my good friends, Diane Bonfert, Cathy Mobley, and Ken Ross, who continue to laugh at my yarns, even when they are only marginally funny.

Thanks to Laura Olrich for helping me navigate the sorcery of computers. I am grateful to the Rocky Mountain Elk Foundation, an outfit that funded the elk restoration in Kentucky, and allowed me to more fully embrace the culture of wildlife conservation.

Thanks to my Mom and Dad who, despite their inexperience in the woods, always encouraged me to keep hunting and fishing. And Maureen, thank you so much for keeping the home fires burning for over forty five years, and for your loving patience while I figured out what I want to be when I grow up.

Table of Contents

INTRODUCTION

I look up and squint. My face is warm in the afternoon sun. Despite the fact that my feet are cold, I am exactly where I want to be. It is late afternoon and I'm sitting on a log with my feet dangling in a stream in the Daniel Boone National Forest, and I am writing in my journal.

It is the peak of the whitetail rut, so today is one of those dual purpose expeditions. I'm wearing waders and my fly rod is leaning against a tree within arm's reach. But, in my backpack is my takedown recurve bow and a tube containing a half-dozen arrows. All morning I've been working my way upstream, casting black woolly buggers to hungry trout. But just around the next bend is a ravine that leads up to a saddle in the hardwood ridge, a place where I know that whitetail deer feed and stage up right before dark. There's a big blow-down on the downwind side of the saddle, a perfect natural ground blind for me to execute an ambush. Or so I hope.

I always loved archery and fishing. As a youngster, I made bows and arrows out of Kentucky cane, and my grandmother taught me to fish as soon as I could walk. When I was eleven years old I was badly burned in a house fire. I spent the whole summer in my small-town hospital enduring various courses of necessary treatment that seemed like endless torture...removing charred skin, dozens of injections every day, skin grafts, cut-downs, learning to live without morphine, and eventually learning to walk after months in bed. Our barber, who owned a shop across the street from my parents' restaurant, regularly brought dog-eared copies of **Field and Stream, Outdoor Life**, and **Sports Afield** to my hospital room, and I read and re-read them until they fell apart. One particular issue had two articles and accompanying photos that caught my eye and sparked my imagination.

There was a piece by Joe Brooks, the legendary fly fisherman, and a photo of him holding a monstrous trout. The other article was by Fred Bear, the "father of modern bowhunting" and was accompanied by a photo of Fred and another hunter trekking across the Alaskan tundra carrying their bows and backpacks laden with large antlers.

I told my Dad, "That's what I want to do."

A quaint custom back in those days was to leave a Mason jar on a shelf in the hospital room so visitors could drop in a quarter, or even a dollar as a gift to the patient. At the end of the summer, when my hospital release was scheduled, my Dad asked me what I wanted him to do with the money. I eagerly replied, "Buy me a bow and a fly rod!" Dad promptly visited the local hardware store and presented me with a fiberglass Ben Pearson 30# bow, a dozen wooden arrows, and a cheap fly rod and reel.

I was so proud and my last few days in the hospital were spent admiring my new bow and waving the fly rod around, terrorizing nurses. My first day home was spent in my backyard, sitting in a wheelchair, shooting arrows at a shoebox and casting with my fly rod.

So began my love for these two implements and their successors. They became the vehicles that have carried me to wonderful places and adventures across Kentucky and North America.

I hope you enjoy this book. Some of the stories are reflective essays, some are "how-to" pieces, and some are just entertainment. Many are stories that have already been published in sporting magazines, but with minor revisions. If you like the book, share it with a fellow adventurer. Hopefully, these stories will inspire you to embark on adventures of your own.

The sun has dropped lower on the horizon and a cool shadow is moving across the stream. It's time to pack up my rod and unpack my bow. I smile, knowing that, deer or no deer, it's been a good day.

Feather Sticks

CHAPTER 1

NA PALI WILDERNESS PRIMER

The best word to describe the hoof print of a Na Pali goat is "delicate." We had spotted goats perched on a high ridgeline, and we just needed to figure out how to make an approach. All we could see was volcanic boulders and ledges too steep to climb without ropes. The main hiking trail circled the base of the ridge, so we pulled on our packs and headed down the trail. It wound through the jungle, crossed a little stream, and climbed in the general direction of the ridge. We followed the trail until it intercepted a goat path. That's where we saw that the mud was pocked with those delicate little tracks, and the freshest ones were pointed up the hill.

I looked at Bradda and he grinned, "Wanna go after them?"

"You betcha," I replied.

We dropped our packs and followed the trail into the green maze. It sidehilled up a ravine for several hundred yards and turned abruptly up the back of the steep ridge.

Bradda looked at me and muttered, "You sure you want to do this?"

"Let's go," I said under my wheezing breath.

So, up we went. And I mean really up. We were on all fours, scrambling through the sword-like sisal and thick vines.

"Thank God Hawaii has no poisonous snakes." I thought.

Several times I slipped and slid backwards, but we inched our way upward, and soon we could see the horizon through the foliage. We reached a small terrace just below the summit and stopped to slow our breathing. I slipped an arrow from my bow quiver and nocked it. Bradda peeked over the ridge crest and quickly ducked.

"There is a goat right there!" he whispered.

I slowly eased to my feet. There was nothing but blue sky and the crashing of the distant surf. I took a step and caught movement to my right. I slowly turned and saw the black billy facing me, trying to decipher my identity. He turned to run, I drew my arrow and anchored....

My hunting buddies know that I love to sit in a tree stand in the autumn woods in Kentucky. I cherish the fall colors, the smell of distant wood smoke, the crisp cool air, and the cadence of a deer's approaching footsteps. I usually sit each location several times before relocating and those tree stand locations become good friends. But, from time to time I like to throw a little variety into my hunting experience.

This adventure began, of all places, in Alaska. Maureen and I met Mike and Judy at a fishing camp near Cordova, where we were limbering up our arms and fly rods on silver salmon. Mike and Judy live in Kauai, Hawaii and we really hit it off, as Mike is an avid bowhunter. Mike invited me to join his buddies on their annual backpack goat hunt in the Na Pali Wilderness. It took a couple of years for me to fit the hunt into my busy work schedule, but here I was, standing on the side of a mountain above the crashing Pacific surf, looking down my arrow at a Na Pali billy goat.

As the goat turned to run I released my arrow. The goat was so close I couldn't tell exactly where my arrow hit, but it felt and sounded solid.

Bradda and I high-fived and he whispered a congratulations. We sat down in the red dirt to give the goat time to expire. Bradda thumbed his walkie-talkie and spoke to Mike who was with the group on the trail below.

"Just shot a billy. May need help tracking."

Then we waited. After ten minutes, the hand-set crackled, "Found your billy. He's dead."

Mike had started to follow our path up the hill, but ran head-long into the dead billy on the trail. The arrow had hit the goat at the base of the neck and angled into the chest cavity, taking out the lungs. It had lived only seconds.

Bradda and I slid down the trail and met the group. We took photos, field dressed the goat, dragged it to a more open spot with a good view, and took more photos. It was a respectable black billy, and I was elated. I thanked my friends profusely, we boned the meat, and loaded the meat, hide, and skull into backpacks for the hike back to camp.

My Na Pali goat.

The NaPali State Wilderness Park is on the northwest shore of Kauai, and is over fifty square miles in area. It lies between the Pacific Ocean and the high peaks north of the Waimea and Po'omau Canyons. The main access is via the Kalalau Trail, that starts at the Haena State Park trailhead. The first two mile stretch to the Hanakapiai beach is frequented by lots of tourists and day hikers. The next nine miles, to the Kalalau Valley, are very rugged, and the trail is appropriate for only experienced hikers. A visitor will encounter endless slick rocks, deep mud, boulders that require climbing, extremely steep slopes, and very narrow trails perched precariously along ledges hundreds of feet above the sea. For good measure, the trail often crosses knee-deep streams and tunnels through a thick jungle canopy that grabs at your gear. Fun? Absolutely! The scenery is reward enough.

Our group camped at mile 6, the Hanakoa Valley, where there is a shelter that makes cooking out of the rain possible. We hunted as far as mile 8. It took over twelve hours of hiking to reach Hanakoa, as we were hunting as we hiked. We encountered many goats, but most were inaccessible, staying on cliffs above the ocean.

The Na Pali goats have lived in this area for over two hundred years, having been introduced by the early European explorers. At the time of this writing, a non-resident hunting license is $105 and a three day Na Pali permit is $20. Both can be bought at the Forestry and Wildlife Division office in Lihue. A Hunter Education card is required. The Na Pali Wilderness is open to bowhunting only. However, from time to time, the state does have a lottery firearms hunt when goat numbers threaten the native flora. There was a firearms hunt about a year before my hunt, but we saw plenty of goats and we all had shooting opportunities.

Here are some Na Pali hunting tips:

Footwear- Perhaps this is the most important piece of equipment to consider. Serious Na Pali hunters wear spiked Tabis, a Japanese shoe with a separate big toe. There are very few places on the trail where there are not slick rocks, greasy mud, or where the trail is not precariously perched above dizzying cliffs. I wore spiked Korkers, fishing boots with interchangeable soles designed to wear over stocking- foot waders. They worked fine on everything but the deepest mud, but they are very heavy. Tabis are goofy-looking but really the way to go.

Clothing - Wear clothes that dry quickly, as it rains a lot and you will sweat profusely. Wear dark color or camo shorts, and a short-sleeve camo shirt. Take an extra pair of dry socks to wear at night. Wear a dark-colored sweat-band on your head or carry a small dark-colored golf towel at your belt. You'll need it to keep sweat out of your eyes. However, pack sparsely, as pack weight is important.

Walking sticks- Always use one. The telescoping staffs with a strap loop at the handle are nice for a bowhunter because you can loop it over your belt knife to free up your shooting hand. A walking stick is imperative for stability and safety.

Fitness- Do not underestimate the challenge of this trail or overestimate your level of fitness. This trail is as tough as most you'll encounter in the Rockies. The only positive is the lack of high altitude thin air. I trained daily for months….jogging, cycling and walking with a full pack, but still I had to rest often. Nothing prepared me for endless climbing over slick rocks. There are several small jungle clearings along the trail that are marked for helicopter landings, but I'm told that the authorities will not initiate a rescue unless the victim is actually injured. In the past, authorities have refused to recue victims that were simply too exhausted to go on.

Meat Care- There are many ice-cold streams along the main trail. The convenient thing to do is bone out your game, put it in nylon meat bags, submerge it in a cold stream to cool it, salt it with rock salt and then hang it in a shady, breezy spot for several hours to shed moisture. Daytime temperatures in the winter are around 80 degrees and nighttime temperatures around 60.

Water- You will sweat constantly, so clean drinking water is important. We used a small filter and Sweet Water purifying drops. This sounds redundant, but Leptospirosis and Giardia could ruin your trip. Carry several water bottles in your pack.

Archery Gear- Bows and arrows suitable for whitetails are fine. Your shots may be long, out to fifty yards, or short, even point-blank. If you shoot a traditional bow with feathers, make sure your fletching is water-proofed, and carry a fletching cover for downpours. Bring bowstring wax and an extra bowstring, as the volcanic rocks and cliff faces are very abrasive. A protective limb tip cover for your lower traditional bow limb would be a good idea as well. Take-down traditional bows or compounds with a short axle to axle length are a real plus, as you can stuff your bow in your pack if necessary or lash it to your pack. You'll have a walking stick in one hand, so having a free hand is sometimes important for safety. On the hike in, I strapped my recurve on my pack, but my lower limb tip was either banging on rocks or my upper limb was snagging on tree branches. It went in my pack on the hike out. If you have to lash your bow to the side of your pack, strap it on the right side of your pack on the hike in, and on the left side on the way out, as there is often a steep cliff on the inland side of the trail. Grease your broadhead blades to prevent rust. Taking extra arrows is up to you. My bow quiver holds four arrows, so I took extras, but I didn't need them.

Optics- The hunting tactic of choice is "spot and stalk." If you bring binoculars, make sure they are light in weight. If you wear glasses, bring them. Sunglasses are optional, as you will be in the shade much of the time.

Packs- Make sure your pack is waterproof, or bring a rain cover. I used a fanny pack during the actual hunting times, but a better choice is to carry your regular backpack, minus your camping gear, when hunting so you can strap your bow to it if you encounter really scary ledge trails. This will also allow you to easily carry boned meat back to camp.

First Aid- Bring a small first aid kit. I included an Epi-pen for severe allergic reactions (there are lots of biting and stinging bugs) and Cipro, a good all-purpose antibiotic . The two items we used most were Advil for constant aches and pains, and moleskin for foot blisters.

Camping Gear- A lightweight tent with a rain fly is advisable. If you are in a group with more than one tent, leave the fly at home and use one tarp over all of the tents. You will not need a sleeping bag, but you will need a bag liner or lightweight blanket. Damp, breezy, and cool conditions at night will make you glad you have something covering your exhausted body. Bring a lightweight inflatable mattress or foam pad.

Share a backpacking stove amongst your group, and use freeze dried meals, jerky, and trail mix.

Game Animals- In addition to goats, wild pigs are abundant in the Na Pali, but primarily nocturnal. We did not hunt them, but still-hunting along "roto tilled" pig trails could be effective. There is also a pheasant-sized game bird called an Erckel's francolin, that we encountered, but got no shots. The wild goats are very sensitive to foreign smells, just like a whitetail deer, and will flee if they catch your scent. Sometimes, over the wind and surf, you can hear the goats. Their bleats sound like a young whitetail. The goats that we heard were mostly lone billies. A good indication of goats nearby is the presence of cattle egrets, big-beaked white birds. They will flock to goats, probably to feed on the insects disrupted from the foliage by the feeding animals. An average billy will weigh around eighty pounds, with trophies weighing more. While these goats resemble domestic livestock, they are wild animals with the same challenges of other sought-after game.

This trip was perhaps the most unique bowhunting adventure I have experienced. I could not have done it without the help and hospitality of my Hawaiian friends. Mahalo!

Author's note: This article first appeared in the August/September 2016 issue of *Primitive Archer* magazine.

Tabis look weird but sure do the job!

CHAPTER 2

GRACE

We like to think we are in control of events in our lives. We script plans, and generally most of us hope we end up more or less where we want to be, doing what we want to do. There are always catastrophic events, like cancer, car wrecks, divorces .things that kick our butts. But generally, we do what we have to do to get the intended results.

That is not always true in hunting and fishing. In fact, if I went back the thirty or so years I've kept hunting and fishing journals, I bet that they would illustrate that beating the odds in those endeavors would be like beating the house in Vegas. I won't do that, though. It might just make me take up knitting or checkers.

I don't always come up empty-handed. I guess the odds are somewhat in your favor when you chase critters for a half century like I have, but, we outdoorsmen come to expect life to tap us on the shoulder and whisper, "Who do you think you are anyway?" We are optimists, hoping for success, but deep down, we are closet pessimists. Hunting and fishing is like childbirth. Maureen and I forgot all of the morning sickness and labor pain when out popped each cute baby. Well, at least I did. That's why we had three.

Ironically, by choosing primitive tools of our trade, like long bows, or feathers tied to a hook, we limit our chances at success, despite buying expensive ancillary equipment, studying maps and moon phases, and sitting in cars and airplanes for tortuous lengths of time to get where we can practice our lifestyle.

Last fall I fished for two long days, pretty much standing in the same stretch of an outstanding trout river, and only caught a couple of small trout. A few weeks later I fished two of the classic trout streams in the East. Holy Waters. I got skunked.

All of these trips were carefully scripted, expensive flies were purchased, leaders greased, waders patched, and licenses purchased. Visions of broad-shouldered trout kept me up nights.

I learned about this phenomenon at an early age. As a pre-teen I was smitten with fly fishing, but I had no mentors. I fished often with my grandmother, but she was a minnow and bobber gal who was pretty good at sitting motionless under a shade tree watching her red cork rise and fall with the waves, hoping it would disappear so she could set the hook mightily on a big bass.

Meanwhile, I would stand on the lake shore a few yards away thrashing at the air with my cheap fly rod. I had read all of the best magazine articles and bought a Boy Scout fly-tying kit. I even had a split willow creel I picked up at a yard sale. I hoped that if I dressed the part and used the flies recommended by the magazines, I would eventually catch fish.

One summer morning we were fishing our usual way. It was hot, and I sat down to drink an RC Cola and rest. I noticed that Granny, who was a smoker, was flipping her cigarette butts into the water. She either didn't notice or didn't care, but every time a lit butt landed on the water, a fish would hit it with a "ker-plunk." Soon the butt would float back up, obviously spit out by the bass. "Hmm. I wonder if I could make a cigarette-fly?" I mused. The next time she finished her smoke I asked her to let me have it. She looked at me like I was crazy but relented. I gently put it out by rubbing it on a rock without damaging the lipstick-stained butt. I poked around in my only fly box and found a single long bluegill hook. I threaded the butt onto the hook and cast it into the lake. Nothing. Nothing happened at all.

"Hmm. What did I do wrong? What was the difference? " I put my best Boy Scout problem solving skills to work, and hit on a possible solution. I asked Granny to light the butt, hook and all. She laughed and humored me, being careful not to hook her own red lips when she inhaled to get it going.

It worked. The little "hiss" that occurred when the lit butt hit the water was the magical fish attractant. On the first cast I caught a two pound bass. Go figure. I had fished in the hot sun all summer, casting the fancy flies advertised in the magazines and I finally caught a fish on a lit cig fly with lipstick hackle. Looking back, I think Granny smoked Lucky Strikes.

One day this past November, I had to do a couple of chores on my hunting property near the National Forest here in Kentucky. I threw some tools in the back of my truck, and just before leaving I looked at my watch and thought I might have a couple of hours to fish a nearby stream, so I threw in my waders, a fly box, net, and a rod. I banged out my chores, grabbed a candy bar and some jerky at a country store and drove the twenty minutes to the stream. Bumping along the gravel Forest Service road, I looked down into the creek bottom. This little stream is usually crystal clear, but I could see that it was a bit murky. Not full-blown muddy, just chalky green. It was 36 degrees on my truck thermometer, and the grey clouds predicted a cold fishless day. I thought about how the water was going to feel through my waders and wool socks, and I shivered. I remembered the last time I fished this stream and couldn't seem to "buy" a fish. I even started looking for a place to turn around. I reconsidered, and thought, "I'm here so I may as well fish. You can't catch anything watching football on TV."

I parked and sat on the tailgate, assembling my gear and wondering about flies. I pondered, "Let's see….stained water, but not too stained… cloudy….there may be a hatch coming off later, but what hatch? A #16 or #18 Adams would be safe…or maybe even a midge would be better." I corrected myself, " Hold on, don't overthink this." I tied on a #11 black bead head wooly bugger, my all-purpose, meat and potatoes prospecting fly.

"If they start rising, I'll switch." I shook my head, remembering my recent luck, and said out loud, "Riiiight." I fished a couple of runs in the shade of the mountain. The rhododendron leaves were curled in the frosty air. No hits. I noticed around the bend that the sun had popped through the clouds, and I could see patches of blue sky.

When I broke out into the sun, I waded into a sweet little sweep downstream of a big fallen log. I was daydreaming and high-sticking the bugger like a nymph, when I realized I had a trout on. I was so shocked that I dragged it straight out of the water onto the bank without playing it or using my net. The trout was around 14" long according to my finger span. It flopped, sand-encrusted, until I could put a knee on it and whack it with a rock.

Once or twice a year, I like to keep trout to eat. We fry them, sautee' them, chowder them, and smoke them. "If I only catch one, I'll eat it for supper. More than that, I'll smoke'm for Thanksgiving." I put the fish on a willow branch stringer, set a big rock on one end, and dangled the other end in an eddy to keep the fish cold. I sat on a log in the warm sun and smoked a celebratory cigar between bites of a Snickers. The temperature was near fifty, the sky was blue, I had caught a nice fish, and life was good. "Okay, let's keep at it," I thought, and I staggered to my feet, grabbed my rod, retrieved my trout, and waded back in.

The next pool swirled around a boulder the size of a Chevy. On the second cast I hooked up, and as I netted the twelve-incher, I thought, "Now at least Maureen can eat one too." Over the next hour and a half I caught more trout, reaching my limit of eight, and hooked three more that I lost. One even jumped three times like a miniature tarpon.

There's a late season catch-and-release section of this same stream that I could have fished after stashing my keepers in the truck, but, it's best not to push your luck. Flirting with too much success borders on greed, which can cause you to break a leg, or drown, or even worse, break a fly rod. That's the Puritan method of fishing. Take the gifts bestowed by God, but don't push it.

A famous fly-fishing writer once said that you'll be a lot happier if your definition of fly fishing depends on poetry rather than body count. However, it is nice to catch a few. There's a certain literary beauty in a golden-smoked trout served with a dill-sprinkled cream sauce and a nice chardonnay. So, there you have it. A two hour fishing trip with no playbook, but more fish caught than on adventures I've planned and agonized over for months.

I used a grand total of one fly. I may retire it, frame it for the wall, and name my next dog after it. Bugger for short. If it's a bitch, I'll name her Grace.

Grace   Granny

CHAPTER 3

Bluegrass Bull

My breath formed clouds of steam in the frosty air in my tent. It was unseasonably cold for mid-October. I unzipped my sleeping bag, retrieved my stocking cap, and wriggled back into my bag. I lay perfectly still, listening. The woods surrounding my campsite were quiet. My camp stove ticked in the dark, cooling off. A bull elk bugled off to the south. Another answered, this time a bit to the east. In my mind I tried to pinpoint their locations, but I knew they would wander in the hours before dawn.

I reflected on how many times in Utah and Colorado and New Mexico I had experienced the sounds of elk in the darkness, the smell of the mountains, the aching muscles of hunting all day in steep terrain, the warmth of a sleeping bag? I was physically tired from the grind of the hunt. But, I was emotionally exhausted from the rollercoaster ride that began late in the summer, and from worry about the elk that I had arrowed late that afternoon.

I thought of my elk hunting "touchstone," Dwight Schuh's book, *Bugling for Elk*. It had been my companion in many planning sessions and in my pack on several elk hunts over the years. Dwight devoted a whole chapter in his great little book to overcoming the emotional ups and downs of elk hunting. Dwight's wisdom had helped me overcome lousy weather, worse food, whole elk herds that had disappeared from the face of the earth, and a friend lost in the mountains. But this was different. These ups and downs were not limited to just this hunt. This had been going on since early summer.

Would this rollercoaster ride stop if I found my elk the next morning? It was hard to believe that I was not chasing elk in the Colorado or New Mexico high country...I was elk hunting in Kentucky.

Before

In late 2005 I booked a northern Quebec caribou hunt with Nunami, Inc. It was to be my hunt of a lifetime. I checked references, watched videos made by several well-known hunting personalities, and I was convinced that Nunami was a topnotch outfit. I paid a deposit, and over the next year I made several scheduled partial payments. I ordered heavier cedar arrows, bought camouflage that would blend in with the rocks and tundra of the Canadian Shield, and I daydreamed of monster caribou as big as moose. Then in May 2006, a payment I had sent was returned unopened. I got on the phone and after several dozen calls to various agencies, brokers, and former Nunami employees, I finally reached Nunami's parent company and spoke to their corporate attorney, who told me Nunami had gone bankrupt. I was told that the company was being bought by another outfitter, and at some point I may get back a small percentage of my money. To date, I have not seen one cent. Not only was I out a pretty sum of hard earned money, but my dreams of a far north hunt were shattered. I was at an all time low. I "hitched up my britches" and decided that I'd only lost green pieces of paper, and that I still had a full season of hunting my beloved Kentucky whitetails ahead.

In March 2006 I purchased my annual $10 Kentucky elk hunt lottery permit. I've bought chances for an elk tag in Kentucky ever since the hunts began six years previous, justifying the purchase by knowing the money goes to a great cause. In 1994 I was the chapter chair for the Bluegrass Chapter of the Rocky Mountain Elk Foundation. At our banquet that year several chapter members, Tom Bennett, then the Commissioner of Fish and Wildlife, and a couple of RMEF officials kicked around the farfetched idea of elk in Kentucky.

To establish protocol, elk were eventually transplanted from Elk Island, Alberta, to Land Between the Lakes in Kentucky. Later from 1997 through 2001, fifteen hundred elk were released in Eastern Kentucky. By 2006 Kentucky had a herd of approximately 6,000 elk in a sixteen county elk restoration zone. The first hunt was held in 2001, with only 12 permits awarded. In 2006, 40 bull tags and 160 cow tags were awarded to two-hundred lucky hunters from nearly 27,000 applicants. Before 2006, several of the chosen hunters had harvested elk with compound bows, but not a single elk had been harvested with a traditional bow.

I was on my way back from my favorite whitetail woods in August when I got a mysterious voice mail on my cell phone. The message was from a good friend and fellow bowhunter, and it went something like this: "You lucky son-of-a-gun! Give me a call...I can't wait to hear all about it!"

I had absolutely no clue what he was talking about! I immediately called him back and learned that he had seen the list of hunters who had drawn Kentucky elk tags on the Fish and Wildlife website, and I was on the list. As soon as I got home I logged on and saw my name. I was naturally suspicious because there are several Bill Carmans in the local telephone directory, so I compared the permit number on the list to the number on the permit in my pocket and they were the same! Yahoo! An all-time high.

A couple of weeks later I received a packet in the mail containing a congratulatory letter and lists of elk-zone wildlife biologists to contact. I immediately got on the phone and narrowed my initial search to two areas. The first was the Dewey Lake Wildlife Management Area. This appealed to me because it is also pretty good whitetail country. The big challenge was the nature of the access. The following Saturday I loaded up a canoe, drove two hours east, paddled two hours down the stream that forms the headwaters of the lake, up a big creek, and I hiked another couple of hours.

From tracks, a couple of sightings, and one far-off bugle, I figured out that the elk were feeding on an adjacent privately owned reclaimed surface mine, and bedding in the forests on the WMA.

I knew I would have a pretty fair chance at an elk, but the sheer distance from my vehicle worried me. Our temperature in early October can reach the eighties during the day. Meat can spoil in very short order.

The second area I considered was in Knott County, near the Perry County line. This was the area of the initial elk stockings, and holds large numbers of animals. However, it is all private land. Dank Crank, the local elk biologist, had arranged for four hunters to hunt on a large tract of old reclaimed surface mine land. I jumped at the chance to be one of those four. I would be hunting with Paul Moore and Jason Richardson, both Kentuckians who had drawn cow tags, and George Timko, a wildlife biologist from Maryland, who had drawn a bull tag. Jason had commitments at home and could not hunt until the second weekend of the season. The three Kentuckians would be bowhunting, and George had committed to at least begin his season with a bow. He was in charge of the Chronic Wasting Disease program in Maryland and would have a hectic schedule in October and November. The Kentucky elk season lasted from October 7 through January 16, but the firearms could only be used during the first week for bulls, subsequent weeks for archery-only cow and bull hunting, and the week of December 9th through the 15th for cows with a firearm..

George and I met Dan Crank in Hazard three weeks before the season to scout. Dan led us up a foggy jeep road in the dark and we pulled over and waited. Soon, as the sun began to filter through the mist, a distant bull bugled...then another...and another and another. There was a symphony of screams, grunts, and chuckles echoing through the swirling fog. We counted at least a dozen different bulls, but we couldn't see fifty feet in front of us. By the time the fog lifted the music had stopped and the herd had drifted into the timber. Dan drove us around the area, showing us the general layout of the land.

I quizzed Dan about the habits of Kentucky elk. Dan told me that like elk in the Rockies, our elk prefer open areas for feeding and forested areas for bedding.

The biggest difference is that our elk have taken on the whitetail's habit of having a relatively small territory. Out west, if you disturb elk, they will run for miles. In Kentucky, bumped elk will run until they feel safe from danger, but will stay in the area in which they feel secure. And, with the smaller areas, while Kentucky elk are still somewhat unpredictable, they have become more creatures of habit, similar to whitetail deer.

Dan explained that the other major difference is the size of the animals. Kentucky elk do not have to survive a ten foot snow pack, migrate long distances to winter range, or adapt to large predators such as grizzly bears or mountain lions. The higher rainfall and sheer green biomass of Kentucky elk habitat, with its lush grasses and deciduous browse, make an average mature bull elk about a hundred pounds larger than his western counterpart.

The property was approximately three thousand acres and consisted of grassy ridges and bowls, and timbered hollows and side slopes. The grassland had been surface mined a decade or so ago and the reclamation had left a wonderful blend of wildlife habitat, perfect for deer, elk and wild turkey. I immediately noticed that at the base of several of the big steep bowls were small cascading streams that were crystal clear, a testament to successful mining reclamation. From a distance, the grassy areas appeared to be green and manicured. However, closer inspection revealed them to be lush, with various native grass species and forbs that were knee deep in most places. Dan, George and I shook hands and parted, excited about the prospects of hunting this wonderful place.

As the season approached and anticipation grew, plans were made to hunt the whole first week of the season, which would be at the tail end of the rut, and to hunt long weekends thereafter. However, I found out that my wife would have to have surgery on the first Monday of the season.

This was a major downer! The surgery could possibly be less invasive with a very short hospital stay, or it could be a major deal. We wouldn't know until the surgery commenced.

I resigned myself to giving the elk the old college try on Saturday and Sunday, and then slipping back down to Knott County when I could get away on weekends between October and January.

I made a personal commitment to take a bull elk with a traditional bow or not at all. I had harvested a cow elk in New Mexico with a compound fifteen years earlier, and had blown a shot at a bull with a compound bow in Colorado. I had drifted back to my roots as a traditional bowhunter, and for a decade I had known nothing else. Several of my non-traditional friends encouraged me to reconsider my decision, as this tag would probably be a once in a lifetime deal, but I've reached a point in my life where what I harvest is less important to me than how I harvest it.

I arrived at our campsite, a beautiful terrace at the end of a half mile jeep track, on Friday. Paul Moore had already set up his tent, stacked a big pile of split firewood, and even set out a target bale. I had spoken with Paul several times on the phone, but we'd never met. Paul is a very experienced hunter, having grown up outside a small Kentucky town and hunted all his life. He is a truly nice guy. His goal was to harvest a mature cow elk with his compound bow. He had been in camp for two days and had scouted the area thoroughly. He helped me set up my tent and unload my gear. We shared stories while I ate a sandwich and we decided to take a walk to stretch our legs and glass some far ridges. We picked our way up the slope above camp and sat down to glass a big ridge to the south. I couldn't believe my eyes! There was a heard of over a dozen elk bedded along the edge of the timber about six hundred yards away, and two were big bulls. We climbed higher on the ridge for a better look. As we wove our way through the clumps of brush, I threw on the brakes and grabbed Paul's arm. Fifty yards above us, just inside the tree line was a huge mature bull. He had his head down, feeding. I couldn't believe it!

Here we were, the day before the season opened, within spittin'
distance of a 6x6 bull elk! We quietly turned and tiptoed back
down the ridge.

We spent the next couple of hours doing camp chores, shooting our
bows, and sharpening broadheads. Just as the sun was dropping
over the far ridge, George came bumping down our little access
trail. He pulled his truck up, rolled down the window, and waved
us away, telling us to keep our distance. Seems his kids had gotten
the flu at school and had given it to him. His drive from Maryland
had been miserable, and he had wisely decided not to camp, but to
get a motel room in Hazard, twenty miles away. We wished him
better health and told him we'd see him tomorrow. He drove
slowly away, his headlights moving across the adjacent hills, his
taillights twinkling red in the clear air.

Paul had staked out a good spot to ambush elk the next morning.
From his scouting observations, they fed in a big flat meadow
about a mile long in the evenings and all night, and filtered back
across a jeep road and up a grassy incline where he planned to wait
in a small copse of stunted trees. He suggested that I climb the
ridge above camp and glass the surrounding hills, hopefully
spotting elk and moving into a strategic location for an ambush.
We turned in early, our spirits high. I woke up twice to the music
of lovesick bull elk.

Opening Day in Elk Country

Sunrise found us eagerly awaiting elk. But as everyone who has
hunted wapiti knows, the one thing you can count on is their
unpredictability. By nine o'clock I had seen nothing except a flock
of noisy crows. I began still hunting the edge of a large open area
to the north, staying on game trails and slipping quietly through the
dew-soaked vegetation. At around ten o'clock, I spotted a lone cow
skylined on a hillside a quarter mile away. Hoping she was the
straggler in a larger herd, I ducked back into the trees and began
jogging around the downwind side of the hill.

Suddenly a small spike bull broke from the timber ahead. He may have seen me or heard me and was attempting to rejoin the herd. I topped a rise and saw it. Approximately forty elk were walking single file along a small ridge, led by a magnificent bull. I threw up my binoculars just as they entered the timber, and my fleeting image was that of a seven by seven monarch, three or four smaller bulls and a big harem of cows and yearling calves. As soon as they entered the trees the bulls began bugling. I trotted toward the ridge and saw George to the south. He waved at me and motioned me forward. Even at two hundred yards he looked bushed. He was carrying his bow like it weighed a hundred pounds.

I eased toward the treeline and found a small nest in the brush that would allow me to stay hidden, but to shoot in several directions. I bugled twice and began cow calling. The response was immediate, and I made ready to shoot. After twenty minutes of calling back and forth, it became apparent that these bulls were not going to risk leaving a bunch of cows in heat. I started stalking into the trees, cow calling every few minutes. About fifty yards into the woods I found a big active wallow, still muddy and smelly. I walked another twenty yards when I jumped a calf, who trotted deeper into the brush. I heard a crash, and looked over the edge of the ridge. Elk, copper in the sunlight, were pouring out of the trees into the valley like grains of corn from a feed sack. In less than a minute, they were a memory. The woods were silent except for the sound of my breath and heartbeat.

I was so impressed with the wallow that I decided to hang a tree stand nearby. I was pretty sure that the elk didn't smell me, so they might be back. I picked out a tree that was strategically near the main trail existing this elk hotspot, and headed back toward camp. It was mid-morning, the sun was high and the temperature rising.

On my way back, I intersected a jeep road and began following it in the general direction of camp. It followed a ridgeline above a big grassy bowl. I stopped to glass the area and saw a bull bedded in the shade of the hillside. He was full grown, but had one antler broken off near the base and everything except his main beam was broken off on the other side. I decided to try a practice stalk. At that time, legal bulls in Kentucky must have at least four visible antler points on one side, but I thought the stalk might be good practice. An hour later I was fifteen yards from the bull. I stood up and waved. He looked at me like he was annoyed and trotted off into the timber. We would see this elk numerous times over the next few days. We named him Gnarly.

Neither Paul nor George had connected. George was so sick he could hardly walk, much less put on a good stalk. Additionally, he would only be able to stay through Sunday, the next day, as his responsibilities with disease monitoring in Maryland had heated up with the nearing of rifle season for whitetails. We conferred and told him that if he chose to hunt with a rifle we would support his decision. Paul even suggested a timbered point where he could build a blind about two hundred yards from a meadow where he had seen several nice bulls.

I ate a hurried lunch, grabbed my strap-on tree stand and headed back to the wallow. As I entered the woods, I saw an elk thirty yards ahead. I froze and took a look through my binoculars. It was a cow, and she was looking the other way. I slowly backed off. Now what do I do? The breeze was gusting, creating quite a bit of noise, and it was blowing from the elk toward me. Could I get a treestand up without spooking the herd? There was a small trail down the slope about twenty yards from the main trail. I tiptoed into the woods on the side trail, knelt at the base of a likely tree and quietly unpacked my gear. I put ten screw-in tree steps in my pockets, unfolded my stand and tied my haul rope to my belt. As quietly as I could I began climbing the tree, moving only when the breeze created cover noise. After forty-five minutes, I was sitting comfortably in the stand with an arrow nocked. It was two o'clock. At two-thirty, a calf elk came walking down the main trail. If there is a calf, I reasoned, then there must be a cow, which meant I hadn't spooked the herd. At around three o'clock I began to see more elk.

Over the next four hours I witnessed something that very few hunters, particularly Kentuckians, have witnessed up close. The whole herd moved to within thirty yards of my stand.

Unfortunately, the October vegetation didn't allow me many shooting lanes, but what I saw and heard was amazing. I heard bugles, chuckles, cow calls, meows, boinks (yes, boinks…Take your cupped hand and strike the end of your grunt tube with your palm, and you'll hear a boink.) I saw bulls jousting and shoving each other. I saw the herd bull mating with a cow. I heard a complete conversation between a calf and a cow. I'll never forget that afternoon as long as I live.

At around six o'clock I heard two gunshots in the distance. "Congratulations George," I whispered.

At around seven o'clock I could tell something was going to happen. The herd began milling around, and finally a big cow walked down the trail that would lead to a shooting lane eighteen yards from my tree. Others began to follow, including two spike bulls, and a very small four by four. I was up and ready to shoot. A respectable five by five started down the trail, followed by the herd bull. I let the five by five walk through my lane. Suddenly a big cow broke off from the line and walked into the brush. The herd bull followed her, and I didn't get a shot. Other cows, calves, and small bulls walked broadside to me at chip-shot range. But I didn't see the herd bull until the whole group was moving across a clearing two hundred yards away. He had been saved by an estrus cow. I waited until it was pitch dark and climbed down. I was disappointed by the turn of events but elated at what I had seen. Surely I would get a shot in the morning when the herd returned to the bedding area. I hiked back to camp in the dark, whistling the theme from "Dances With Wolves."

Paul and I arrived in camp at the same time, full of stories. About to be busted by a bull, he had taken a hurried shot at a cow and missed. Our spirits were high. It was only the first day of the season and we were into elk big time!

We fixed supper, and waited for George, anticipating that he had shot an elk and may need assistance. The full moon climbed into the autumn sky, and I shot my bow by moonlight. Not needing to see the target through a peep sight like my companion, I was putting arrows in a tight group at fifteen yards. Paul and I built a big fire, opened a couple of cold beers and toasted Octobers past, Octobers present, and Octobers to be.

Where was George? At ten o'clock, we drove out to the jeep road nearest where he had been hunting and pulled the truck over next to George's. We shined our flashlights into the night air, whistling. I even tried a bugle, but was answered only by a distant lonely bull. We thought we saw a flashlight flickering on the mountain, but realized it was the light on a distant cell tower. We drove silently back to camp, our spirits dampened. At eleven o'clock we turned off our lanterns wondering if he was lying somewhere in the woods with a broken leg, or even worse, shot. At midnight I thought I heard a truck's engine. I held my breath in the dark, listening. I unzipped my tent flap. It was not my imagination. George's truck was coming up the path. Paul and I climbed out of our tents, pulling on pants and jackets.

George had shot a big six by seven bull with his rifle at about two hundred yards. It had staggered a few steps and he anchored it with another shot. He had spent nearly six hours skinning and quartering the beast. Luckily, the temperature was supposed to be in the high twenties overnight. He had spread out the big chunks of meat on rocks to cool. We all agreed to meet in the morning after a couple of hours of hunting to help haul the meat the half mile hike to the nearest jeep road.

Paul and I climbed back into our tents. I don't remember going to sleep, but I distinctly remember waking up to the sounds of Paul's dishes clanking in the dark. It was time to get at 'em! I heated coffee and ate a couple of sweet rolls, packed Snickers and Gatorade in my day pack and headed for my tree stand. I was trembling with excitement.

I just knew that the big herd bull, the king of the mountain would walk right down the path by my setup. I was already planning for the taxidermist, the freezer full of elk, the stories to tell.

Day 2   A Close Encounter

I was in my stand well before daylight, and I was able to experience the ritual of the Kentucky woodland dawn. The woods came alive slowly. First a barred owl welcomed the first hints of grayness with his deep "who-cooks-for-you" call that all turkey hunters have heard. Then from a point way down the mountain I heard the soft yelp of a wild turkey still on the roost. A crescendo of small whistles and chirps built as the wrens, chickadees and cedar waxwings welcomed sun. I heard the staccato sound of a deer walking in the leaves off to my right. Try as I might I couldn't see the deer, but I imagined it was a regal buck. The smell of the pine forest and organic leaf duff mixed with the smell of rutting elk. The whole experience was intoxicating. But, no elk appeared. If I hoped it, willed it hard enough, they would appear, walking down my trail. But they had vanished. After all, they were elk.

At ten o'clock, I climbed down and walked back toward camp, dejected. Another day on the rollercoaster. My path took me by the area where George shot his bull. I fully expected to spend the remainder of the morning packing elk quarters out of the hills, but his truck was nowhere to be found.

When I came trudging into camp, Paul was chewing on a piece of jerky. His luck had been similar, but he had at least seen elk. A herd of about twenty, with several bulls, had fed onto the back of a big wooded mountain to bed for the day. They were on a natural terrace trail, and Paul thought he would set up an ambush where they went into the woods. He hypothesized that if they stayed on the same level and didn't come out where they went in, they might be vulnerable to an ambush where the same terrace came out on the far side of the mountain. Was I game? I didn't have a better plan, so I thought I'd give it a try.

"What about George?" I queried? "Did he get his meat out?"

"He started hauling meat at daylight, and I pitched in at around nine o'clock, but there was only one load left."

I felt bad about not pulling my weight, and I hoped I would see George before he left.

I ate lunch in silence and began packing up my camping gear. I mulled over what my afternoon plan would be. I would break camp, load my truck, and hunt until dark. I knew that I would be limited to only very high probability shots if afforded the opportunity, because I was due at the hospital in Lexington with my wife early the next morning. Given the sheer magnitude of getting a dead elk out of the woods, there would be little time for blood trailing.

An hour of disassembling, rolling, stuffing and boxing gear left an empty, lonely space where my portable home had been. The only sign if its existence was a rectangle of matted grass.

Paul and I conferred, and we decided to drive our trucks as close as we could to the area where the elk were bedded. We lurched and bumped our way to the jeep road. I looked back at our campsite, wondering if I would be back.

Halfway up the road we met George's truck. He had driven back into the area to say goodbye. His truck was completely loaded with coolers full of meat. He fished around in the back and pulled out a huge six by seven elk rack. The brow tines were as long as chair legs. I took a picture. The elk rack outlined his face like a frame in a frame. He was tired but happy. He figured he would drive two or three hours toward Maryland and crash in a cheap motel. I wished he had felt better, could have shared our campsite, and could have bowhunted longer. He is a good man.

We arrived at a big pile of gravel on the jeep road, a remnant of the surface mining activities. We both pulled our trucks over and shut off the engines.

We got out and stood, our hands in our pockets, looking over the big grassy bowl below us. It was a beautiful fall afternoon.

The hills were beginning to turn, and tinges of red and yellow highlighted the dark greens of the oaks and pines. A hawk winged overhead in front of a big puffy cloud. After a few moments of silence, Paul muttered something like, "This makes it all worth it." We stood a while longer. Paul cleared his throat and pointed out a little clump of trees that marked where the terrace trail exited the woods. I told him I would meet him at dark at the trucks, we said our "good lucks" and I began picking my way down the slope. I looked back and Paul was walking south on the jeep road, his bow canted casually over his shoulder.

I made my way down the slope to the terrace and found a distinct elk trail. I followed it past the clump of trees to the edge of the woods, and stood, listening. Were the elk still bedded? I pulled a cow call out of my pocket and blew it softly. I waited. Nothing. I blew it again, only louder. Suddenly, from across the valley, a bull bugled. Could the whole herd have walked off the back side of the mountain, crossed the creek, and gone up the side of the far slope? I cow called again and got an immediate response.

"Off to the races!" I thought, as I started down the slope, cinching the waist belt on my daypack. I decided to take the shortest route to the bottom, so I angled into the woods toward the sound of the bull. The terrain was extremely steep and I had to slide and grab onto branches and roots to keep from falling. At the bottom I found a well-worn trail that wound its way along a stream. I had to move branches out of the way as I moved along the trail and I wondered how an elk with wide antlers could navigate through the brush. But, there were rubs on the saplings everywhere.

I stopped to catch my breath and listen. Something scampered up the slope across the creek. It could have been a squirrel, or a deer, or an elk. The dry leaves magnified the sound of every movement. I blew my cow call again. A bull bugled on the terrace behind me, up near where I started. Now what? I cow called again. Another bull bugled to the left of the one I had just heard.

The herd was obviously still in the woods on the terrace. I turned and started back up the slope, shaking my head, moving fast.

The breeze was blowing down the slope in my face and I could smell the sweet barnyard smell of lots of elk. Soon, several bulls were bugling and the herd seemed to be on the move. I picked up my pace, trying to get ahead of the herd. Suddenly I saw movement in the trees above me. A large brown form floated slowly, right to left. I caught a glimpse of antlers. I ducked below the lip of an embankment and blew the cow call. The bull screamed a hoarse bugle and the trees seemed to shake. I backed slowly down the slope until I was hidden, then I ran up and to my left. I grabbed small trees to pull up the slope, digging my toes into the clay for traction. My breath and my heartbeat deafened me. Sweat poured over my eyes. I continued to climb, wiping sweat with my forearm. I topped an embankment and saw a big tree blown down ahead. I circled it, trying to find a place to hide. There was a hollow behind the roots and I knelt, slipped off my daypack, and drew my bow twice to make sure I had room to shoot in the general direction of the elk.

I cow called again. Another bugle erupted from the trees ahead. The herd bull walked slowly, almost deliberately toward me. He was about fifty yards away, walking with his head down. His antlers, each probably four feet long, were swaying back and forth like antennae. He stopped at thirty-five yards and began rubbing his antlers on a small tree. I softly meowed on the cow call. He looked at me, staring right through me. He again walked forward, cautiously. At twenty yards he stopped behind a clump of sweetbriar. I froze, putting tension on my bowstring, knowing the moment of truth had arrived. If he stepped clear of the brush I would have a shot. He stood for an eternity, not moving. He then simply turned and walked straight away up the hill. I sat down in the dirt and tried to put my arrow back in my bow quiver. I was shaking so hard I had to use both hands to guide it.

I finally caught my breath and looked up. The sky was azure blue, framed by the tops of towering pines. Another bull bugled way above me, and I could smell the elk and the pines.

"Unbelievable," I said out loud. "Unbelievable." Montana or Wyoming could not have been any better. "Unbelievable."

I shouldered my pack and continued up the slope. The bugling had stopped, but I could still smell elk. I was now on the terrace trail, moving toward the opening into the large grassy bowl. It was beaten muddy by large hoof prints. I slowed down, putting one foot gently in front of the other. I could now see the big meadow sloping up toward the jeep road. There were approximately thirty cows and calves and four bulls grazing in the sun on the side of the hill. The composition was perfect as if it had been posed for a painting on a wildlife calendar.

I knelt in the shade of a clump of sumac at the edge of the woods and blew my cow call. One of the bulls turned and took a step toward my position. I called again, hoping. Suddenly a calf broke away and galloped like a racehorse right toward me. It skidded to a halt no more than ten feet away, and stood, inhaling deeply to determine what manner of elk I was. I reached behind me for my pocket camera, slowly raised it, and snapped a picture. The camera clicked and the rewind whirred. The calf barked and wheeled away. I had gotten a picture, but I was busted. The whole herd ran across the hillside and into the timber.

The woods were quiet. The sun was low and I knew I had less than an hour before packing it in. I took a swig of Gatorade, ate half a candy bar, and stood up, stretching and sore. I hiked up to the road and walked in the direction of camp.

"I'm here," I thought. "I might as well act like I'm hunting. You never know."

I cut across a weedy field full of grapefruit-sized boulders. At times I had to walk with my arms spread like a tight-rope walker to keep my balance on the broken ground. I soon came to an old logging road. I turned and started back toward my truck.

The sun had now dropped below the horizon and I knew I had thirty minutes of legal and practical shooting light left. I had put the arrow I usually carry in my right hand back in the quiver when I crossed the rocks, and I had a fleeting thought that I should get it back out, but didn't.

The was the "gloaming," the best part of the day, my favorite, the time when the diurnal animals move toward their dens and nesting sites, and the nocturnal animals casually begin to move from bedding to feeding grounds. The woods are quieter, and the air cooler. I turned up the collar of my jacket, and enjoyed the experience, remembering the weekend's events, almost daydreaming. I started around a large clump of low brush when a very large bull elk stood up, twelve yards away, and stared at me. I grabbed for an arrow, but he stampeded over the hill before I could even get it out of my quiver. I had made a beginner's mistake. I hadn't been ready. I shook my head in disbelief and walked back to the truck. The first weekend of Kentucky elk season was over.

My wife's surgery was successful and relatively uncomplicated. We went home the same day, and we were relieved and thankful. The lure of the elk woods was pulling at me. However, my mother developed a severe infection which put her in the hospital on Tuesday. The next two days were spent in the hospital rooms, talking with doctors, eating hospital food, and a late night move from one hospital to another. The rollercoaster was screaming downhill. Elk hunting wasn't even on my radar screen.

On Thursday, my daughter called and offered to come home from college for hospital duty. Additionally, my brother and his wife were due back in town and could help. Everyone told me not to worry. Go elk hunting. On Thursday night I threw my gear back in my truck and by the pre-dawn hours on Friday morning I was headed southeast toward the mountains.

Day 3 Back in Camp

My plan was to arrive in Knott County just before daylight. Just east of Lexington I was delayed by a pileup on the interstate that cost me a half hour. I drove faster, trying to make up time, but the forty miles of crooked roads between the Mountain Parkway and the elk woods required a much safer speed, and as I topped a ridge on Ky. 80 just west of the turnoff to the jeep road, the first rays of sun poured through my windshield. I rationalized being late by deciding to go straight to my wallow tree stand, theorizing that the elk wouldn't drift down the ridge to bed for several hours. I parked my truck near the turnoff leading to my campsite, closing the doors quietly to minimize noise, and I hiked up the road toward the ridge. I veered into a quarter mile wide field we called "forestry flat" because of the surveyor's flags marking new tree seedlings. There was a trace of a trail leading east toward wallow ridge and I followed it. I crawled up to the top of the rise overlooking the ridge leading to the wallow and I fished my binoculars out of my pack. I turned the focus knob and four cow elk materialized, grazing just at the edge of the woods. I was too late. Elk were already moving onto the ridge.

I backed off, wondering what to do next. "One thing's for sure," I thought, "I'm not going to bust those elk out of the bedding area."

I decided to still-hunt some new territory for a couple of hours before setting up camp. I prospected several likely looking groves of trees along the edges of the thick forests, places that were textbook elk habitat, with no luck other than running into Gnarly, who eyed me with suspicion, and a noisy flock of wild turkeys that erupted from a thicket like a covey of quail. I made my way back to the truck and drove to my campsite.

Paul had broken camp and left two days earlier. He had passed up marginal shots at a couple of cows, knowing he had three months of elk hunting left in the season.

He was due back in camp on Monday. I would be able to hunt Friday, Saturday and Sunday before work and family commitments would pull me away from this remarkable place.

Jason Richardson was due in camp that evening. I had spoken with him on the phone and he told me he would be accompanied by his father and brother and they would be in a four wheel drive pickup pulling a large RV camper. They were worried the rig wouldn't make it up the mountain, so as an alternate plan they decided they could camp in the Walmart parking lot in Hazard twenty miles away if the road was too rough or steep. I was glad I was traveling light. My camp site was beautiful.

I set up camp, pitching my tent in exactly the same spot as before. Like the whitetail, I am also a creature of habit. It was a breezy sunny day, but cold weather was predicted for that night. I hauled two big coolers into my ten by twelve tent, setting my two-burner stove on one and my lantern on the other. I would be able to roll out of my sleeping bag in the morning and start coffee while I dressed. My little campsite was cozy and starting to feel like home. I made a sandwich, opened a soft drink, and ate slowly while I shot arrows into a target bale I had placed at the base of the mountain twenty yards from my tent.

My left shoulder had developed a dull pain and soreness that hurt more when I raised my bow arm to shoot. But it was no worse than the other minor aches and pains associated with my traipsing around the countryside, climbing hills, trees and wading in creeks. My shoulder hurt, but so what? I blew it off.

After some mental debate I decided to hike back to my wallow tree stand. In theory, if the wind was right, I would be able to slip into my stand and catch the elk undisturbed. I made the one mile hike, glad to be hunting. As I topped the ridge above forestry flat I felt the wind over my left shoulder, the opposite of what I needed to hunt the stand. I circled to my right and crept along the edge of the woods until I was just short of being directly upwind of the wallow. I knelt in some brush and found a rotten log to sit on.

I spent the next few minutes gingerly trimming twigs and small branches so that I could raise, draw, and shoot my bow in the direction of the main trail leaving the woods.

From the evening hunt I had experienced the week before, I knew that the elk were probably bedded on the ridge behind and to the left of the wallow. If the wind held steady, they would leave the bedding area on the trail twenty yards in front of me, and I would have a broadside shot. I pulled on a camo face mask, nocked an arrow and settled in to wait.

I immediately began to hear the chirps and meows of cows and calves, right where I hoped the herd was bedded. I glassed the surrounding ridges to pass the time. A big blond coyote ran across the barren hillside a quarter mile distant, the breeze moving its fur like wheat in the wind.

An hour passed and the wind was steady. I saw movement through the trees. A large cow elk walked up the trail and entered the field right in front of me. I slowly lowered my head so the shadow of my camo ball cap would cover the glint of my eyes. She paused momentarily to look at me, not seeing anything but a strange lump in the landscape. She continued along the trail, feeding in the scrub grass at the edge that led toward my position. I tried to keep my eyes on her and the trail without moving, hoping she would entice a bull to follow. She fed closer and closer. Soon, she was ten yards away and closing. She stopped ten feet from me and stared, her ears up, her big nose quivering. I tried not to move, not to blink. Suddenly I could see the realization in her eyes. She wheeled, barked, and crashed into the timber. I heard large bodies breaking limbs and the pounding of hooves.

The evening's hunt was over. I pulled off my face mask, and stuffed my binoculars back into my pack. The hike back to camp was easy, mostly downhill. It was dark when I arrived and I felt my way into the tent and to my lantern like a blind man.

I had a message on my cell phone from Jason. The hill was too steep and they were at the Walmart.

I heated venison chili and sipped a beer, listening to the coyotes in the distance. Steam was rising off of my chili and as I blew on it between bites. I knew it would frost heavily that night. I fluffed up my down sleeping bag and dug out long underwear from my duffel. I finished eating and turned out the light early, wondering if tomorrow would be my lucky day.

Day 4 Success?

The next morning there was a furry white coat of frost everywhere. I was gathering up my gear to leave camp when Jason and his companions drove up. We all shook hands, reaching through the open windows of their pickup. Their faces shown with anticipation in the dim light of the truck cab. They wanted to hunt on the far south side of the property where there were several big knobby hills to sit and glass with binoculars. We agreed to meet for lunch and we wished each other luck.

I decided to drive out to the rock pile and hike the big north-south ridges, probing the tree lines and seams in the landscape with my binoculars, I had walked about twenty minutes when I spotted a lone bull elk silhouetted on a far ridge. I moved a bit closer and saw four more bulls below him. The wind was blowing right to left, so I circled the hillside on my left, hoping to get downwind but uphill of the bulls. It worked and soon I was kneeling in a clump of weeds about seventy five yards above the nearest one. He was our old buddy, Gnarly. I knew he wasn't the smartest critter in the woods, but it wouldn't take much to spook the others, so I sat there and waited. Finally, Gnarly fed off to the left and over a rise, but by then the other four had walked down into a big hollow. There was a small four by four bull, a very large five by four, a five by five, and a huge six by six. After an hour I was within forty yards but I had run out of cover. Forty yards was too far for me and my recurve. They finally moved into the same woods where I had encountered the herd on Sunday afternoon.

I reasoned that they would probably bed on the back of the hill and move out of feed on the terrace trail, just like the whole herd had done when I called in the calf. I immediately formed a plan to be nestled in the brush near the terrace trail when they came out that afternoon.

While I was hiking back to the truck I spotted a big cow elk feeding at the top edge of the forestry flat. I went on to my truck and decided to try and find Jason. If the cow would stay put, he may be able to try a stalk.

I found Jason, his dad, and brother at the top of a big shady knob. They were sitting, enjoying the autumn sun, and looking through binoculars at every rock and stump that could be an elk. I told them about the cow elk and they were enthusiastic about trying a stalk. His dad would watch and his brother would videotape the hunt.

An hour later found me perched on a rock a quarter mile from the fat wapiti. The Richardson's had circled downwind and climbed up the steep embankment to the lip of the ridge. I could see Jason and his brother creeping from rock to rock. It was like I was watching a movie unfold before me. His dad was peeking over a big boulder with binoculars. His brother was on hands and knees holding the video camera at head level, trying to film the stalk. I saw Jason raise his bow and I saw his arrow fly like a gleam of light. The elk bolted thirty yards and stood perfectly still. Moments later its back legs buckled and the elk was down.

We spent the next several hours skinning and quartering the big cow. Jason was a happy hunter and his family was about to participate in the post-hunt rituals. I took a picture of Jason and the elk. His smile made my day.

As the Richardson's drove away, loaded with elk steaks, I looked at my watch and knew I'd better hustle. It was two-thirty and I was completely out of food and water. I hurried back to camp, wolfed down a sandwich and a bottle of Gatorade. I took a few practice shots with my sore arm, and headed back to the terrace trail.

When I reached the rock pile I began negotiating the steep slope into the grassy bowl. I was halfway down when I saw the two bulls. They were bedded in the shade of a small clump of bushy trees near the edge of the field. I immediately dropped down in the tall grass. I peeked through the weeds with my binoculars. The elk were lying, facing away from me, their heads up, chewing grass. I squirmed out of my backpack, pulled on my face mask, and began crawling down the slope toward the two elk. When I was forty yards from them I realized I was only fifteen yards above where the terrace trail snaked out through the meadow. If the bulls fed out into the field on the trail I would have an easy shot. So, I waited, kneeling in the tall grass.

After fifteen minutes, the two elk stood up in unison, and began walking back toward the woods. When they went behind the clump of trees, I sprinted forward, trying to close the distance. At twenty yards, the lead bull walked out from behind the trees. He paused, quartering away. I picked a spot low behind his shoulder and released an arrow.

The shot looked good as it whipped over the top of the tall grass, maybe a bit low and a bit forward, but good. The bull lurched forward and both elk ran to the edge of the woods and stopped. The trailing bull was blocking my view of the elk I had shot. I sat down in the grass and waited.

"Go down! Go down!" I whispered.

I waited for what seemed like hours, but was probably only a minute. The two bulls simply walked out of sight into the woods. I was puzzled. The shot looked good but I couldn't be sure. I crept along the terrace trail toward the woods. I found the back third of my cedar arrow painted bright red with blood. I eased forward with another arrow nocked and ready. Where the two elk had stood I found a small puddle of blood. I walked another twenty yards into the woods and decided to back off, terrified I would spook a wounded elk, never seeing it again.

I remember nothing of the hike back to camp. Replaying the shot over and over in my head, the flight of the arrow, the posture of the animal, the color of the blood, I was back in camp without knowing how I got there. I knew the twenty degree temperatures overnight would preserve the meat, at least until mid-morning, but I was sick with worry. I could barely eat. I crawled into my sleeping bag, lying in a fetal position, shivering. This is where this story began. I unzipped my sleeping bag and reached for my stocking cap. My breath formed clouds of frosty steam in my tent. My camp stove ticked in the dark, cooling off. Would the rollercoaster ride stop if I could find my elk in the morning?

Day 5   Another Chance

The night's sleep had been fitful. I had dreamed of arrows flying in the dark like birds. I was up early, drinking coffee. I loaded my truck with the gear necessary to manage a downed elk and I drove to the rock pile. I climbed down the slope to the terrace trail just as the sun's rays warmed the far mountain. I walked to the blood spot and began still-hunting the trail. I found one more blood spot fifty yards past the first. I began to think like a mortally wounded elk, avoiding obstacles and uphills. I followed the trail all the way around the mountain, finding no more sign. Then I followed several side trails that led downhill toward the creek. I thoroughly searched the thickets along the creek. As time passed and the air warmed up I became more and more concerned. Panic began to gnaw at me as I frantically searched the woods, almost running. I was no longer looking for a blood trail. I was looking at every log and rock, hoping to see the elk lying in the leaves. By eleven o'clock I had covered the bottom three-fourths of the mountain and I was exhausted. I needed a rest. I hiked to my truck and drove back to camp, pondering what had happened.

I am not a good shot. Or rather, I am not *always* a good shot. With a traditional bow, one with no wheels, cables, pulleys, or sights, the archer shoots instinctively, much like throwing a baseball.

To be consistently accurate, one must not shoot at the target, but at a small spot on the target, like a tuft of hair or a small discoloration, or imagine a nickel lying in the perfect spot on the animal. When I can keep my wits, I pick the spot and usually harvest the animal. However, sometimes in the heat of the moment, particularly when events aren't playing out as expected, I shoot too quickly without focus and I shoot poorly.

I have made a couple of embarrassingly long shots at game animals, and despite the fact that they ended up in harvests, they were unethical and I regretted attempting them. And I have missed my share of short shots. Just last year I missed a twenty yard shot at a 160 class whitetail and thirty minutes later I easily made a perfect shot at a doe that was standing in exactly the same spot on the trail.

With all of that said, when the two bulls disappeared behind that clump of trees and I sprinted forward to close the distance, I *did* keep my head. When they stepped out I focused on a spot behind the lead bull's elbow and I thought the arrow dropped over the weeds in exactly that spot.

I have been seriously bowhunting since I was fifteen years old. In all of that time I have never been as low as I was that morning. I was within a hair of wrapping my bow around a tree and burning all of my arrows.

As I grimly ate lunch and began packing up camp for the trip home, I formulated a half-hearted plan to break camp and head back up the mountain. I would give the search the rest of the day before driving home. I owed that much to the animal. .

I sloppily stuffed my gear in the truck, cramming odds and ends into my meat coolers. "Packing well and leaving room for meat will surely bring me bad luck," I reasoned sourly.

As I drove away I didn't look back. I probably wouldn't be back whether I found the elk or not.

I parked at the rock pile and started down the slope. I left my bow in the truck. It was noon and I knew I would either find a dead elk or nothing at all. But, something made me turn back to retrieve my bow.

"Be prepared," I thought.

I climbed into the bowl and walked down the trail until I found the last blood. I stood there thinking, "What would a mortally wounded elk do? Where would he go?"

I looked around in all directions. The only direction I hadn't checked was straight up the slope to the top of the mountain.

"What would a *non*-mortally wounded elk do?"

There was the faint scuff of a trail leading up the slope through the brush. I started up, holding onto limbs of small saplings. The trail widened and began to switchback to gain topography. Halfway up I was hanging on to a tree, trying to catch my breath, when a red shine on a rock caught my eye. Blood. I continued up the trail toward the ridge, using my bow as a walking stick in the steepest places.

As I neared the top I could see sky and I knew the ridge was close. I slowed down and gathered my wits. This was a new game altogether. I was hunting again. I eased over the ridge. To my left was a large grassy clearing and ahead the forest edge circled back and away. I stood, looking. Fifty yards away I saw movement. I knelt down and retrieved my binoculars from my pack. I focused and saw a bull elk feeding on some low-growing brush. I took a slow step to my left and could see more of the animal. There was a shiny wet spot on his upper front leg. The mystery was solved. I had shot low and my arrow had sliced his leg. From his movements, the wound appeared to have had no ill effects on the animal.

The breeze was right to left and at times almost windy. The sun played over the red and yellow leaves like a kaleidoscope when they moved with the breeze.

I began shifting my position, moving only when the breeze kicked up. After fifteen minutes of oozing forward I was within twenty five yards of the bull. He looked as big as a house. I took one more step and waited. The breeze moved like the mountain had exhaled, and I shot the elk perfectly. He wheeled and ran, crashing down the hillside. I walked over to the edge and looked. He was a hundred yards down the slope, piled up, dead. This time I had been prepared.

I slid down the slope to the elk. I took off my hat and sat in some ferns. Now what? My mind was racing, trying to decipher what had just happened. I had actually tracked down this bull elk and killed it with my bow. There he was, right there. Touch his antlers if you think it's a dream. His coat was smooth. I stroked his nose like I would a favorite saddle horse. He was beautiful.

I removed four things from my pack. The first was a turtle shell and in it was a package of dried Sioux sweetgrass. I wanted to thank God for this amazing gift but wanted to do it in a way that was befitting the animal and the way it was harvested. I poured the dry sweetgrass into the turtle shell and lit it with a match. White smoke plumed up and I set the shell on the ground next to the bull's head. I knew that his body heat, his very existence, was rising with the smoke up through the autumn leaves.

Next I removed a cigar that had been given to me by friends. "If you kill an elk, smoke a cigar." they said. I lit it and puffed, smiling.

Next I pulled out my camera. I shot a whole roll of film that afternoon, but I took the first picture by wedging the camera in the fork of a tree and setting the timer. In the picture I look like I was in shock. I was.

The fourth thing I removed was my knife. It had served me well over the years and this was the day it was made for.

It took seven hours to cape, skin, quarter, and haul the elk to my truck a half mile away. I was completely exhausted, but the rollercoaster had stopped.

My elk was a 5 x 4 bull. I estimated his live weight at around seven hundred pounds. He was the first elk, in modern times, harvested with a traditional bow. He wasn't what some would call a monster, but I sure was happy.

My sore shoulder had been a partially torn rotator cuff. Wrestling elk quarters finished the job. My doctor asked me if it was worth it. Absolutely.

Paul Moore spent several weekends in October and November hunting for that big elusive cow. He finally harvested what probably was the herd matriarch. We met at his company office just before Thanksgiving to exchange pictures and tales. We stood in the parking lot, braced against a cold wind, talking about our adventure, sharing something that very few people have experienced. It was hard to shake hands and say goodbye.

I looked like I was in shock...I was.

Authors notes: An abbreviated version of this story first appeared in the April-May 2008 issue of **Traditional Bowhunter Magazine**. Back in 2008 I could not have predicted the impact that this hunt would have on my life. I saw my first elk while in grad school in Utah in 1976. I had been a volunteer for the Rocky Mountain Elk Foundation for several years in the early 1990's, and I had hunted elk with modest success in several western states. When I retired from my long-term career in 2007, I applied for a job as the KY-TN-WV Regional Director for the RMEF. As I'm told, the competition for the job was stiff, but having successfully hunted elk in Kentucky gave me an edge, and I got the job. For nearly ten years I worked with a group of outstanding volunteers and wildlife agencies in those states to support the elk herds, and I was involved in initiating the elk reintroduction in West Virginia. I retired from the RMEF in May of 2017 and I now have an elk/bear hunting and fly fishing outfit (www.kentuckywildoutdoors.com) that allows me to help other hunters and anglers achieve their outdoor dreams.

CHAPTER 4

Nectar

I'm not much of a drinker. Oh, I may have a beer with a bowl of chili, and I occasionally crave a particular concoction or another if the mood strikes me, but despite my addictive personality, my genetics did not predispose me to regular drinking. So, when I happened upon the ancient bottle of whiskey, I'm not sure why I drank it.

My buddy, Tom, and I were fishing the south branch of Michigan's Au Sable River about three miles downstream from where vacation homes start to crowd down to the river and lawn chairs and pink plastic flamingos sprout from its banks. We were lazily wading a wild stretch of river that appeared virtually untouched and undisturbed. I half expected to see a wolf or a moose.

It was a cool September day with a cloudless bluebird sky. We were catching scads of trout on tiny Adams and fur ants. We had stopped and plopped down on a large log to rest, eat sandwiches, and smoke our customary mid-day cigars.

We sat and talked and marveled and I lay back in a patch of green grass. Something bumped my legs that were dangling in the current. An old algae-covered bottle ebbed in the current. I picked it up and rubbed it against my waders. As the green came off the bottle, I could see its faded label and I realized that it was a half pint of Scotch whiskey and the remnants of the paper cap seal were intact. It was still full.

Tom and I looked at each other.

"What'd ya think?"

"Go for it!"

I twisted open the cap and took a long sip. The liquid was trout-stream cold, but warmed as it filled my mouth. I handed the bottle to Tom and he took a tentative sip, and then a longer one. We both lay back in the grass, puffed cigars, talked about shared experiences and we drank Au Sable Scotch.

That's not the only aged drink I've enjoyed, compliments of Mother Nature. Several springs ago I was scouting the farm I've been hunting a quarter century. There's a twenty acre cedar thicket that I prefer to leave undisturbed during the whitetail season, as it is a core bedding area. But, it was spring and there was ample time for spooked deer to settle down before September. So, I was walking around, looking at tracks, old rubs, and hoping to find a shed antler or two, when an odd shape and color caught my eye. A large stump was nestled into the forest floor just high enough to sit on, and surrounding it was a pile of old beer cans.

Several years earlier I had met an old codger (now deceased) on this farm who was gathering walnuts. He gave me some valuable tips on deer locations. Later the farm owner told me the old fella enjoyed releasing his coonhounds and sitting in the woods on moonlit nights, listening to dog music and drinking beer. It seems I had found his favorite listening post.

There were literally hundreds of crushed beer cans piled up and scattered around that old stump. I hiked back to my truck and retrieved a box of plastic garbage bags and began cleaning up the mess. The deeper I got into the pile, the older the cans, and on the bottom, the labels had completely faded off.

The tops had stubs from those old style pop-tops, and many of those old metal tabs littered the ground as well. I filled up three or four garbage bags and was picking up the last few cans scattered about. Then I discovered an un-opened can. The brand name had long since faded and the lid was old school, so I knew it was decades old.

It had been a cool spring morning but it had warmed up considerably, and I had broken a sweat picking up and hauling aluminum. I held the can up to the sunlight, grinned, and popped the lid. It foamed perfectly, and no beer has ever tasted better. I could have saved it as a souvenir, but the experience was worth far more than a beer gathering dust on a shelf.

I'm not above drinking non-alcoholic antique beverages. When I was younger and considerably slimmer, I was on a bicycle road racing team. One day, on a fifty mile training ride, I stopped at an old country store out in the middle of Kentucky farm country to rest and quench my thirst. I picked out a can of Mountain Dew and set it on the counter to pay. The guy at the register eyed my purchase and said something like "Ya like Mountain Dew do ya?"

"Yep", I replied, "It's my favorite."
He stepped from around the counter and said, "Follow me."

I followed him into a dark back room. He pulled a string and an overhead light flickered on. He opened the top of one of those ancient steel chest coolers, the ones where you insert a dime and slide the drink through a little gate and down a track to the opening. This one was humming and clicking like an old Ford. He slid a bottle along a chute and lifted it out of the cooler. It was a greenish-yellow, very dusty, and had an early hillbilly logo. It was an authentic vintage Mountain Dew. I could see that rich orange and lemon sediment on the bottom of the bottle. Beautiful.

"How much?" I asked.

I would have given him twenty bucks, but he said, "Fifty cents, just like the new ones."

I walked out of the storeroom and held it up to the light. It had begun to collect condensation and frosty drops were sliding down its surface. I paid him and he produced an old "church key" bottle opener from his pocket. It was the best Mountain Dew I ever tasted. Apparently 1970 had been a fine year.

Occasionally I'll actually use spirits for medicinal purposed. I was once on a four day backpack deer hunt and developed a severe toothache. Seems the only relief I could get was a good gargle of Kentucky bourbon. You can bet I didn't spit it out. That would have been a waste of good medicine.

When I'm on longer wilderness adventures, the collective creative minds of our expeditionary force can usually concoct a refreshing and appropriately named beverage. For instance, there's the Boundary Sour, invented deep in Minnesota's Boundary Waters Canoe Area Wilderness. The ingredients are 2 cups of cold lake water, 1 tablespoon of powdered lemonade mix, and 1 shot of Kentucky bourbon. It is guaranteed to soothe sore legs and shoulders, and it goes well with a good cigar.

Then there's the San Juan Sour, enjoyed best at 11,000 feet in the Colorado Rockies: 2 cups of cold snowmelt; 1 tablespoon powdered Gatorade; 1 shot of tequila. Warning: Do not try these recipes at home. They don't taste nearly as good. It must be the clean air, or maybe wood smoke.

The oldest beverage I ever tasted was not a one hundred year old scotch or a Rothschild wine. It was several thousand years old. The heck you say. Last year my wife, Maureen and I went on an Alaskan Cruise and afterward we rented a car and bummed around for a week, fishing and sightseeing. We visited an interpretive center near a famous glacier.

Right there in the building was a table where two college interns had placed a cooler-sized slab of blue ice, dug from the base of the calving glacier. I broke off a small corner of ice and put it in a paper cup to melt. As it melted, I sipped water that may have contained pollen from plants eaten by wooly mammoths, or touched by paleo-Indians. It was a warm autumn day, and the water tasted pretty good too.

One of the stupidest things I ever drank tasted the best. ("And these other things aren't stupid?" you may ask.) It was the mid 1970s and I had started grad school in northern Utah. Frankly I was more interested in deer and trout than grades and a thesis, and early September found me deep in the Bear River Mountains with a big mule deer buck I had arrowed. I was fairly new to the challenges of the mountains, and I had no food, water, or pack frame. I was four miles from the nearest trailhead, and started dragging the 200 pound beast at 10 a.m., reaching my car at 9 p.m. It was a warm day, but the trail paralleled a crystal clear stream. I drank from its cold water several times, but paid the price. I later discovered that I was a couple miles downstream from a large herd of sheep. I got a bad case of giardia and had the runs for a month. Stupid.

I am older now and wiser. I carry plenty of water and a water filter in my pack. But I usually leave a side pocket in my pack empty, just in case I happen upon a liquid treasure. I want to be ready to take advantage of an opportunity to broaden my repertoire. You never know what might float your way.

The source of glacial nectar.

CHAPTER 5

THE JUMPER

When I shoot a deer it rarely drops in its tracks. I have, on a few occasions, spine-shot a deer that collapsed on the spot. But that is rare. Most of the time, the shot itself marks the beginning of another hunt, finding my arrowed deer. It can be challenging, often enjoyable, and sometimes frustrating.

The first thing I do is attempt to note a landmark along the deer's flight path that will enable me to start deciphering the blood trail. Then I replay the shot and the deer's subsequent behavior in my mind. Did he bound away with his tail up? Did he hunch up and run with his tail down? Did he stumble and favor one leg? Did I hear him fall? Did he run a few yards and stop? Answering these questions often will often direct me in that next phase. Then comes the waiting. The customary thirty minutes seems like an eternity and, depending on the deer's behavior and shot placement, that thirty minutes may stretch out to several hours or more. Finally, I begin solving the blood trail puzzle. With the two-blade broadheads I normally use, penetration and lethality are outstanding, but blood trails are sometimes sparse. To satisfy my overwhelming impatience and curiosity, I often walk quickly ahead, trying to avoid disturbing the blood trail, scanning the forest floor for a dead deer. If after a few minutes I don't find my prize, I return to that initial landmark and start the tedious blood trailing job. Every episode is a learning experience.

In 2003 I shot a deer, and I can only call that experience bizarre. It was one of those beautiful autumn afternoons. I was sitting in my favorite tree stand enjoying the fall landscape, the cool breeze, and the sounds and smells of rural Kentucky.

My stand was perched in a big oak tree growing at the edge of a steep fifty-yard embankment above a wooded terrace where an old logging road snaked along the bluff over the Kentucky River.
 Below the logging road terrace, the drop to the river was almost vertical, and was covered with downed trees, scrub brush and big rocks. There was a subtle dip in the ridge where I sat, like a small saddle. Deer often used that little topo relief to climb up from the terrace to the woods, and that ambush spot had proven itself many times over the years.

About a half hour before dark that evening, I heard a twig snap behind me. I slowly swiveled my head and caught movement. Two bucks appeared on the terrace. One was an exceptional deer, a big ten-pointer. Ahead of him was a very nice big-bodied eight-point buck. I immediately decided to shoot whichever deer presented an opportunity. The lead deer climbed from the terrace, walked right under my stand, and stood broadside about ten yards in front of me. I was terrified he would spot movement if I tried to stand up, so I decided to remain seated. My bow was already vertical, the lower limb tip resting on my foot. I eased my bow up, picked a hair behind his shoulder, drew, and released. The deer exploded and bounded fifty yards along the ridge. Then he just stood there. The target had been way to close to follow the blurred flight of the arrow, so I had no clear idea where it struck the deer. The animal continued to stand, craning its neck, trying to determine the source of the muffled twang of my bowstring.

Puzzled, I began scanning the ground beneath my stand for my arrow. I immediately spotted the red fletching. The arrow was lying on top of the carpet of leaves , the point facing me, just beyond where the deer had stood. It appeared clean and blood-free. I looked back at the deer. He began slowly walking down the embankment toward the terrace. His gait was a bit off...not exactly a limp, just a bit out of rhythm. He reached the terrace and quickly lay down. Now I was really mystified. My arrow appeared clean and unbroken. Did I miss? Surely not at ten yards. The buck lay still but his head was up and alert.

I decided to wait and let the encounter play out, rather than risking a sixty yard shot at a deer that I wasn't sure I had even hit. After ten minutes or so, he got on his feet and walked over to the rim of the bluff. He took another step and jumped. Like Superman.

I heard his big body hit a ledge and I could hear limbs crashing as he rolled and slid down the slope. It sounded like he made it several hundred yards before he stopped. The woods became quiet.

I shook my head. What the heck? I gathered up my gear, lowered my bow, and climbed down to examine my arrow. The broadhead was broken off right where it had been glued to the cedar shaft, and was missing. The arrow appeared to be clean. I ran my finger over the broken tip. My arrows are stained walnut brown, so it was hard to be sure if there was blood. I smelled the broken tip. All I could detect was the odor of the cedar. If there was any blood, there sure wasn't enough to get excited about. It was getting dark. When in doubt, back out. Besides, I did not relish the thought of climbing down that bluff in the dark.

The drive home was a cacophony of country music on the radio and the voices in my head. Should I get someone to help me in the morning? Is the deer dead ? Where did my arrow strike him? How could two inches of penetration with no obvious blood kill a deer? Where is my broadhead? Should I fetch a canoe? Maybe I could paddle down the river to a spot below my stand to avoid bringing a dead deer up hundreds of yards of very steep and tangled terrain.

I decided to call my buddy, Tom, to get his advice. He offered to come back with me at daylight to help retrieve the deer. So, just as the sun's rays popped over the horizon, we were standing at the edge of the terrace, stomping our feet in the cold, peering with binoculars down toward the river, trying to catch a glimpse of a dead deer. Tom spotted a sliver of white underbelly through the foliage. Now the work began.

We slid down through the rocks, dead timber, spider webs and stickers. The deer was splayed out, wedged against the trunk of a tulip poplar. I grabbed a front leg and pried him loose so I could examine him. There was a small slit low in his front shoulder, just above his brisket. We rolled him over and re-wedged him so he wouldn't continue sliding down the slope. I field dressed him as quickly as possible, stopping only to examine the heart. Yep, there was a hole right through the center of it. I fished around inside his body cavity until I found what I suspected. The broadhead was embedded on the inside of his off-side leg. Mystery solved.

Photo by John Sanders.

Where the jumper jumped.

The arrow had hit low on his near-side, passed through his heart, and stuck in the far leg, where it sheared off when the deer bounded, pushing the arrow back out so quickly that what little blood had been on it had been rubbed off by hide and bone. That deer had lived a good ten minutes with a hole right through his heart. Why the buck jumped off of the bluff is anyone's guess.

Using a rope and lots of elbow grease, it took us several hours to wrangle that deer to the top of the slope. We should have fetched a canoe. We dragged him out to the pasture where we took a couple of snapshots, loaded him in the car, and headed home to finish the butchering.

The lesson learned? If I hadn't seen that deer jump and heard his careening slide down the slope, if I had only seen him lie down, get up, and walk off, and, with no blood and little evidence that I had killed that deer, I would have surely been tempted to give a half-hearted effort in trailing him. And maybe I would have given up, chalking that one up to a bad shot and a non-lethal wound. I would have been dead wrong.

So, when blood trails are fading and complicated, I think back to the Jumper. His last act on this earth has made me a more persistent and patient finder of arrowed deer.

Last year, I remembered the Jumper and put the lesson to good use. I was sitting in a tree stand between a little oak ridge and a clover patch. I could shoot either spot. Often, deer will feed on acorns and then move over to the clover for dessert. I had seen a very respectable buck earlier in the year, had hunted him hard, but he had eluded me. It was early December, the rut was winding down, and I decided to change things up. Rather than my normal evening sit, I arrived well before daylight. It was a frosty morning, and my steaming breath clouded the air in the glow of my headlamp as I walked down the logging road to my ambush spot.

By 10:00 a.m. I had just about given up hope. I enjoyed the songbirds flitting around the edge of the clover patch. I called in a fat hen turkey that had been yelping in the distance, using my voice to fashion two soft clucks. She quit yelping and appeared fifteen minutes later, wandering back and forth across the ridge, looking for her buddy. Unfortunately, she offered me no shot opportunity, but I did get a kick out of watching her antics.

The sun was warming my chilled body, and I was half asleep, musing how much longer I should stay in my perch, when I saw movement at the edge of the clover. A small basket-rack six point buck walked out of the woods across the clover and began feeding. Soon he was joined by a big doe. I watched them for about thirty minutes, wishing the big boy I had been hunting would also arrive. He didn't. When the doe walked into a shooting lane I shot her. As she ran across the opening and up into a pine thicket I was horrified to see my arrow dangling and flopping from her side. It appeared as though I got very little penetration and had hit her way too far back. I sat down and muttered a few gosh darns and shook my head. What the heck had happened? I just knew I would never find that deer. But I needed to do everything in my power and go through all of the motions pretending that she was dead. I remembered the Jumper, and how he had apparently sustained a non-lethal wound, and how I was wrong in my assessment of that shot.

So, I waited two hours to take up the trail. I followed scuff marks in the leaves into the pine thicket, and found a little tunnel through it where she might have gone. I found some unidentified scratch marks in the dry dirt where she may have crossed the logging road, and I found more leaves disturbed on the other side. I was walking where a deer might have walked, but I was walking on faith alone.

Finally I found blood. About a tablespoon's worth was splattered on the dry leaves. So far, my intuition was serving me well. But now I was at a crossroads. The deer could have gone straight down to a creek bottom, she could have angled obliquely to the right, toward an area in which I knew deer often bedded, or obliquely left, toward higher ground. First I went straight down. The leaves were all scratched up by turkeys looking for acorns, so I couldn't see any clear sign of the doe. A hundred yards of tacking back and forth across the face of the hill resulted in finding no obvious sign. I returned to the blood and turned right, following a deer trail toward the bedding area. I followed it for a quarter mile, crossed the creek and angled back upstream.

I was splitting my attention between scanning the ground in front of me for blood and scanning the forest for a dead deer. Nothing.

I returned to the blood and sat down. I had been looking for two hours for a deer I was now sure was just wounded, not dead. I got down on my knees and peered at the blood spatter. The deer had been standing still and there were no tell-tale directional splashes. I looked closely at every drop. I then noticed a small drop that had the faintest little smear pointed to the left, up the watershed. "Okay. Let's start over," I thought.

I shouldered my day pack and began slowly walking toward a funnel where two big deadfalls almost came together, leaving a four foot gap. The leaves were disturbed in that gap. I eased through it and found more leaves that had been kicked up. The trail angled down to the only logical place to cross a steep little ravine made by a side creek. There was a mark on the other side where something had slipped in the mud.

I examined the mark, but couldn't identify the maker. I climbed up to the top of the narrow finger ridge. Another crossroads. The logical route would be straight down along the spine of the ridge. I followed it for a hundred yards when I saw a shiny red spot on the leaves. I stood there, wondering if it was simply a wet red oak leaf, and I was reaching down to pick it up, when I saw the back of my arrow lying on a brown rock. I took another step and realized the rock was a dead deer.

Field dressing the deer revealed that my arrow had hit the deer high and back, but at a severe quartering angle. It had penetrated the deer's liver, the far lung, and had barely popped through the skin behind the far leg. The deer's fleeing motion had sheared off the broadhead. The arrow had essentially bounced back out, creating the illusion that very little penetration had been achieved.

I also discovered something else. My doe was not a doe. "She" was a young buck that had already shed his antlers. Why in the world a buck would lose them that early in the year is a mystery.

Without my experience with the Jumper, I may have given up on the deer. The arrow that shot the Jumper sits on his antlers in my office as a reminder that when I'm tempted to abandon a deer's trail, I should stay with it just a bit longer. Things are not always what they seem and events don't always play out as expected.

Author's note: An abbreviated version of this article appeared in the Summer 2017 issue of **TradArchers' World** magazine.

CHAPTER 6

BEACH BARBEQUE

My wife, bless her heart, loves the beach. She adores the sun, surf, salt air, children and grandchildren making sand castles, smiles, cold drinks on the beach....you get it. While I enjoy the relaxation associated with a week in the surf with my family, frankly, after about day three I'd rather be hunting.

Last spring I was wandering around the National Wild Turkey Foundation convention in Nashville when I ran across a booth for a deer lodge located near my family's planned summer beach getaway. The outfitter told me that booking an early July hog hunt would pretty much ensure me the run of the whole place, so I took him up on his offer. I would sneak away from the hordes of children for a couple of days and deal with hordes of mosquitoes. Sound fun? You bet! Actually, the weather was cloudy and breezy, there were very few mosquitoes and there were hogs-a-plenty.

Our beach retreat was in coastal North Carolina, and in that state feral swine are treated like varmints with no special seasons and with no special big game stamps needed. The area I hunted had crop fields interspersed with woodlots, all surrounded by creek bottoms and swamp land. The owner had a number of tree stands left out from deer season, so I perched myself in a pine tree near a trail intersection for the first evening. I saw several pigs moving toward their feeding grounds, but couldn't pull off a high probability shot. Late the next morning I started a stalk on some oinkers along a small creek, but realized they were feeding toward my previous evening's stand, so I circled ahead of them, climbed the tree and pulled off a double lung shot on a perfect one-hundred pound "eater" boar.

Like many of my generation, my first exposure to wild hogs was the Disney movie, "Old Yeller." The star of the film, a mongrel yellow lab mix, saved a young pioneer boy from being mauled by feral swine, but the pigs infected the dog with rabies. The climax of the film was a weeping boy shooting his own dog.
The film painted a nasty picture of wild hogs, and to some degree, it was accurate. They can be aggressive when agitated, and they do sometimes carry diseases.

Wild hog hunting is as much a part of Southern culture as okra, grits, and cornbread. However, of late, hog hunting as a sport has found itself embroiled in a controversy that reaches across all states where wild pigs roam. Wild hog hunting in the South began in 1912 in Graham County North Carolina when a British company represented by George Gordon Moore imported a group of wild Eurasian hogs and released them into a poorly fenced preserve near Hooper's Bald for hunting. These hogs escaped and may have bred with domestic feral swine. The populations of wild hogs in the Smoky Mountains in Tennessee and North Carolina are direct descendants of those Eurasian hogs and have a distinctive humped shoulder, shaggy mane, and long snout. Most of the wild hogs further south and east in the coastal states are mixtures of feral swine and hogs brought to the New World by Spanish explorers in the 1500's. In an odd twist of fate, some records indicate that the large populations of wild hogs in California originated when that same George Gordon Moore actually moved some of the Eurasian pigs from North Carolina to Santa Clara County and released them.

While wild hogs are fun to hunt, and make excellent table fare, they are extremely detrimental to wildlife habitat and agricultural interests. They are omnivorous, and will eat anything from corn to wild turkey eggs, to crayfish, to citrus fruit. They root in fields and streams causing erosion and fouling the water with excrement, and they compete with our native wildlife for forage. They do occasionally carry diseases that can spread to livestock and humans.

On top of all that, they are prolific breeders, with sows producing up to twenty five youngsters per year. They are the most prolific large animal breeder in North America.

Because of the threat to wildlife habitat and agriculture, many states are waging war on wild hogs, using helicopters, night vision technology, and large steel cage traps. Captured hogs are generally not relocated to better environs....they are destroyed. Most agencies do not contribute the meat from these animals to food banks, due to potential disease problems and the practicality of hauling out large numbers of carcasses. However, on private properties, landowners often request the meat, and the agencies comply.

Kim Delozier, retired Wildlife Biologist for the Great Smoky Mountains National Park, is a wild hog expert. He started working for the GSMNP back in 1978 as a seasonal wild hog hunter. Living in the backcountry for days at a time with nothing but a rifle and a backpack, he would kill hundreds of hogs per season. Kim is a big soft-spoken gentleman who is now the Eastern U.S. Conservation Program Manager for the Rocky Mountain Elk Foundation. To illustrate the serious nature of the hog problem, Kim Talked about hog numbers in the Park.

"The Park Service is beginning to make headway in hog management. They now kill two to three hundred a year. In 1986, with about the same effort, there were over 1,100 hogs removed from the Park. The numbers, thankfully, have been reduced to a maintenance level."

"Hogs are smart critters. Ranking land animal intelligence based on brain size, primates are on top, bears second, and hogs third."

The emerging philosophy is that the more wild hogs are valued as game animals, the harder it is to control or eradicate hog populations.

Common sense would imply that the more popular wild hog hunting is in an area, fewer wild hogs would be in that area. However, research and experience has shown that in areas where wild hogs are a popular game animal, they are actually illegally trapped and relocated by hunters, outfitters and lodges to spread the populations and hunting opportunities. The recent spread of wild hogs to at least thirty-eight states has been directly linked to translocation (sometimes illegal) of wild hogs to fulfill a growing desire for local hunting opportunities.

Tennessee is among a handful of states that have banished wild hogs from its list of game animals, and made it illegal to sport hunt them, trap them for relocation, possess live hogs, or transport them. Tennessee is trying to control the hog population by stopping illegal transportation, and enabling landowners to obtain exemptions to use any means of hog control, night or day. While there is no more legal "hunting" of wild hogs in Tennessee, there actually are more opportunities to bag a wild hog in areas currently populated by them than ever before, and a hunting license is not even required.

Chuck Yoest, a biologist and Wild Hog Coordinator with Tennessee Wildlife Resources Agency, says this about TWRA's hog control program, "The two largest challenges have been meshing the enforcement of our laws against illegally transporting wild hogs with the need to allow transportation of hogs that appear to be wild hogs, such as the "heritage" breeds, by legitimate breeders. The other challenge in controlling wild hogs has been mustering the resources needed to combat such an enormous problem. It takes a lot of money and cooperation among different agencies and sportsmen."

In nearby Kentucky, wild hog hunting is essentially non-existent. Hogs began to appear in the 1990's, and a focused effort on a small population made eradication efforts more effective. Hog hunting has never been a significant part of Kentucky's hunting culture, and probably won't due to the small number of the critters.

Chad Soard, the wildlife biologist for the Kentucky Department of Fish and Wildlife Resources Wild Pig
Program at the time of this writing, is happy to report that Kentucky is currently "ahead of the game."

"We recognize that stemming the release of hogs must arise through a disinterest in hunting them."

In the last three years, Kentucky's program has eradicated 600-700 wild hogs, but there are still a few breeding populations left in Kentucky.

"Our biggest challenge has been inconsistencies in the pressure applied. Eradication demands science-based implementation across property boundaries. We may have several adjacent landowners who are experiencing damage from hogs who are very cooperative in allowing a tactical approach to eradication. But then there is the one nearby landowner who may experience the desire to hunt them and will not cooperate. His land then becomes a hog sanctuary."

So, the war continues. Meanwhile, back at the beach, many coastal states embrace wild hog hunting as an economic benefit that helps control nuisance animals. The coastal Carolinas, Georgia, Florida, Alabama, Mississippi, Louisiana, and Texas all have healthy wild hog populations controlled to some degree by hunters, alligators, bears, panthers, and in Florida, large exotic snakes. Finding a place to bowhunt wild hogs near a beach suitable for a family vacation is as easy as a click on the computer. Google search "wild hog hunting in (the state of your beach destination)" and you'll quickly discover multiple opportunities, ranging from lodges to do-it-yourself opportunities on public land.
Hunting wild hogs with a traditional bow has a high probability of success by waiting downwind of a trail to a food plot or crop field. Hogs have marginal eyesight, so stalking is effective if you are camouflaged, quiet and downwind. Hogs are vocal and groups can be located by their grunts and squeals.

A word of caution: Hogs are tough and even a well-placed arrow may still result in a long and nasty blood trail in a swamp full of snakes, insects, and all manner of prickly vines.

Older hogs have a gristle "shield" around their shoulders, and their lungs sit further forward than deer, so an angling forward shot behind the shoulder is your best bet.

State laws governing wild hog hunting change from time to time, so make sure you consult recent state hunting regulations before planning your hog hunt. The decision to hunt wild hogs is more complex than simply going hunting. Should we participate in an activity that may, in the long run, be detrimental to our wildlife resources? Or should we, where it is legal and appreciated, embrace our hunting heritage and do our small part in harvesting these critters? I suppose the next time my family heads to the beach, I'll have to make a tough decision whether or not to pack my bow with the beach umbrella.

Recipe for Beach Barbequed Wild Hog Ribs

Rub rib racks with your favorite BBQ dry rub. Put in large baking dish with 1 beer and 2 cups water. Seal tight with aluminum foil. Leave in 250 degree oven for 2 hours. Remove, and coat ribs with your favorite BBQ sauce. Put on the grill and turn regularly until the sauce is browned and the ribs steaming. Eat with some rice or potatoes, fruit, cheese, and red wine. Southerners prefer including coleslaw and green beans cooked with onions until mushy. The southern beverage of choice is sweet tea, but I like a frosty beer or glass of red wine.

Author's note: This article first appeared in the June/July 2014 issue of *Traditional Bowhunter Magazine*.

My Beach Hog.

CHAPTER 7

WILDERNESS JOURNAL 1997

I absolutely love the North Woods, so I couldn't believe it had been nearly a decade since I had been to the Boundary Waters Canoe Area Wilderness. My eldest son, Dan, was nine years old then and he accompanied me. This year he couldn't make the trip. Starting college as a scholarship wrestler means lifting weights and running and farewells to girlfriends, things that preclude trips with Dad. I vowed, however, to spend at least one night sleeping on the same ground we had slept on nine years earlier.

On that first trip, back in 1988, Dan and I had picked up matching sticks that had been stripped clean by beavers to take home as souvenirs. Somehow, though, we had lost both of them before the trip was over, and I vowed to replace them this year. So, my buddy Tom was to be in the bow and I in the stern. Tom has been my bow man, both literally and figuratively for many years, spotting hazards and keeping me on course. We borrowed a sixteen foot lightweight Kevlar canoe with portage yokes, and chose to begin our journey from Sawbill Canoe Base on the eastern edge of the wilderness. We knew that Sawbill had fishing licenses for before, and the admirable combination of cold beer and hot showers for after.

We had mulled over maps for months and had chosen the Lady Chain – Louse River Loop, which would take us deep into the wilderness. The Lady Chain refers to a half dozen lakes named after the spinster aunts of an early explorer. Each of the women had distinct personalities as do each of the lakes.

"Louse" sounds uncomfortably like "lost" when said quickly. We planned to be "Louse" for at least a week.

Transportation in the Boundary Waters, unlike the great wilderness areas of the Rockies where horses are the norm, is limited to canoeing. The canoe carries you and then you carry the canoe and so on and so on. Also, unlike other wilderness areas, the isolation is serious isolation. For instance, in the Flattops Wilderness in Colorado, if someone falls and breaks a leg, a companion can jog or hike or ride a horse out for help in a matters of hours. In the Boundary Waters, there is no quick way out. If you are three days in, it takes three days to get out and cell phones don't work there.

We packed out gear to double-portage between each lake. One trip was for carrying our regular backpacks with sleeping bags, stoves, tent, and the like. The second trip would be for the canoe and the food pack. Grizzled Boundary Waters regulars can comfortably handle single portages by carrying the backpack on their back, and the Duluth Pack, which is a big waterproof duffle with straps that goes on your front. We had visions of broken ankles and blown-out knees, and opted out of Duluth packing. So, we did every portage twice...there, back, and there again.

Portages are measured in rods on the BCWA map. A rod is sixteen feet. Whoever devised this system had some experience in psychology. Ninety rods sounds much shorter than one thousand four hundred forty feet. We loaded our little craft and shoved off from Sawbill on Saturday morning at 10 a.m.

Day 1

We turned north from Sawbill base, paddling down Sawbill Lake and portaging an easy eleven rodder through the forest to Kelso Lake. The sounds of the activities – weekend canoeists, car campers, sightseers – around Sawbill diminished like ripples from a pebble dropped in a pond. The sun warmed my neck. Had I remembered my sunscreen?

A big bird, probably a blue heron, flew and disappeared, gliding around the point of an island. We paddled hard for an hour and stopped to fish and rest. No bites. Two men and a young boy paddled alongside and spoke of seeing a moose and the promise of northern pike. We pushed on toward Lake Lujenida. I cast a big weedless spoon into some reeds and started my retrieve. The line jerked and went limp. I reeled in northing but line and air. The line was cut clean, probably by a toothy northern. I put my small spinning rod under the gunwale and pulled out my casting outfit with fourteen pound test line, the big gun, and tied on a silver buddy. It worked. In Lujenida, we caught several small northerns, but threw them all back. The last thing we needed was extra weight on the next portage, the longest we would have on the whole trip. Low water had stretched it to over 500 rods, more than a mile and a half, a total of four and a half miles of being a pack mule. We ate lunch and had at it. Our food pack was still full and our legs were still accustomed to only sidewalks and lawns. We left considerable sweat in the trail dust.

The portage ended in Zenith Lake. It was five o'clock and we were bushed. We made camp, ate, and swatted mosquitoes. It was humid and still and smelled like rain. I crawled into my sleeping bag and dreamed about the poacher who had crashed a plane on Zenith back in the forties. He had walked to Tofte, thirty miles away, in the snow in his street shoes. I woke up once, and the crunch of his icy footsteps became the flapping of our tent fly in the night rain.

Day 2

We awakened to fog and the anticipation of hot coffee. I hadn't slept well.I never do on the first night,and the coffee helped. Our first portage was a 92 rod downhill trail. As we reloaded our boat, three canoes pulled up; five teenage girls and a young man who looked like he'd been pistol-whipped. He had beaded corn-row hair braids. I imagined him being held down by five howling girls and being forcibly braided.

They were Girl Scouts and had been out for two weeks. I think he was ready for male companionship and a Marine haircut. They told us of seeing a wolf on Mesaba Lake, three portages west.

We turned our craft west and paddled until noon. Mesaba was picturesque and a high breezy rock offered a bug-free campsite. We cooked lunch, swam and lay in the sun. Toward dusk, Tom caught a small sunfish and rigged a pole with live bait. After gazing at the motionless bobber for an hour, it disappeared with a plop, and the line was parted cleanly. Probably another northern. We longed for a steel leader or two. At dusk, a bald eagle flew over camp and turned its head, watching us suspiciously. That night we slept to the sound of waves lapping at our beached canoe.

Day 3

Our third day was the hardest yet, having seven portages. We paddled the lengths of Chaser, Dent, Bug, and Tool lakes and parted seas of colorful water lilies on the rivers between. We were moving deeper into the wilderness, a paddle stroke at a time. The portage trail to Bug Lake ended in a swamp. The water was only a muddy two or three inches deep. We were puzzled. Surly there was an alternate route. We retraced the trail and a third of the way back someone had built a cairn of rocks on a flat boulder to the right. A faint trail led over the hill and we followed it. It wound its way over a high ridge, and as we crested the hill I looked over at the vista, a sea of green forests and slate blue lakes, shining like coins on a carpet. Tom raised the bow of the upturned canoe on his back like a beak and stood, looking.

Bug Lake was big and lonely. Its shores were lined with flat rocks. We beached and as we made lunch, I looked across the landscape. The vastness of the word, "wilderness" struck me. No cars, no planes, no people, just the woods, the lake and the blue sky. We could have been in Alaska. Tom took a nap while I lazily fished. I finally lay back in the bed of moss under a spruce tree, dozing. The breeze caressed my face.

We both were awakened by the splash of ducks landing on the lake. We packed our cook gear and headed for Trail Lake.

As we paddled out of the backwater into Trail Lake, we saw a canoe, the first in nearly two days. A man and presumably his wife paddled toward us. She seemed upset, scowling back at him. We hailed and asked them where they were headed. He said Malberg Lake. She shook her head, and off they went. Tom and I looked at each other. The guy's nuts. Malberg is six portages and at least six hours away, and it's already five o'clock. Oh well. We made camp on a high rocky point. A curious chipmunk kept us company during supper, begging for granola. That evening, as we cast for pike, a river otter floated on its back around the point just beyond camp, nibbling on a crayfish.

Day 4

It was again foggy at dawn. The fog was a nice way to gradually reveal the landscape every morning. The sky and the lakes and the sheer vastness of the wilderness were better given to us in the small doses as we sipped coffee and planned the day's expedition, rubbing the ground-kinks out of our necks.

Tom caught a chunky northern on the way to the first portage, where we sliced it into pan-sized filets and dropped it into a bag of cornmeal to keep for lunch. The morning's portages were boulder-strewn and we had to go slowly, picking our way delicately over rocks and under deadfalls. The river wasn't much wider than the canoe in some places. Twice we dead-ended at beaver dams where we dragged the boat over the moss-slick jumble of cut sticks. It looked like no one had been on this route for a long, long time. We cooked lunch by a waterfall on a tiny unnamed lake. The fried pike was a welcomed change from the jerky and granola we normally had for lunch.

At the end of the next portage we found a campfire, dead but still warm. The fussing couple must have made it that far, giving up for the night.

The waterway grew even smaller, the rocks and logs scratching at the canoe. We came around one of the endless twists in the stream and startled a cow moose as she stood shoulder-deep in the green pool. She slowly walked up the embankment, trailing water lilies like Christmas lights, looking back at us out of the corner of her wide glaring eye. She turned and vanished into the timber.

Finally, we reached Malberg Lake. It was big and blustery. We turned the canoe toward Lake Koma, our goal for the evening. Near the portage we met a family of three in a large canoe. We gave them the thumbs up just as I snagged another northern pike. I was too tired to clean it, so I dropped it overboard, still thrashing. I swear it actually tried to bite me as I released it. Next time, buddy, you are fish sticks.

The portage to Koma was mostly uphill, the first all uphill portage since the big one on Day 1. The trail wound upward through the trees alongside a splashing stream. The map described dangerous rapids and advised not to float the stream. Now it was too shallow to float even a toy boat. Koma was fishy. We caught northerns, smallmouth bass, and walleye. We paddled to within thirty yards of a bald eagle perched on a snag eating a fish. I wondered if it were the same one we had seen at Mesaba. Two long days of Lewis and Clarking for us was probably only about fifteen minutes for the eagle. He flew away when Tom took his picture. Certainly not a publicity hound. We ate supper, fished until dark, and fled into our tent swatting at swarms of hungry mosquitoes.

Day 5

We were up at dawn, coffeed, and loaded early. We wanted to fish a good spot we had found the previous night before leaving Koma. We each caught a walleye, and Tom filleted them on the blade of a canoe paddle, a Boundary Waters "cutting board." I threw one fatty skeleton onto the rocks for the birds and Tom released one into the current. The sun's reflection made the ghost fish look almost like it breathed and finned away. I moved slightly and could see it drifting downward, upside-down, small pieces of flesh waving against the rocks.

The three portages to Lake Polly, the first sister, were hot and dusty. We met a solo canoeist with state-of-the-art equipment. He told us of a nuisance bear that was stealing food from packs at the portages a bit further south, near Lake Kawishiwi. Tom and I looked at our food pack, and remembered the five-hundred rodder. "He can have it!" we said in unison.

Polly was a wild and forlorn lake with steep, wooded cliffs and cold deep water. We voted not to fish, but to plow on as we still had a very long day ahead. Just before the portage, Tom cast toward a rocky point. I called him a wuss who couldn't take the temptation, but I gave it a try as well. No luck.

Polly to Lake Phoebe involved a narrow stream with six portages, two of them over a hundred rods each. Tom carried the canoe on the first three, and I took the last. We were getting much stronger. Last Saturday, a hundred rodder was a killer. Now it was Thursday, and it was routine.

Nine years ago, Dan and I camped on an island in Phoebe. One of the best nights of my life was on that island. I remembered good food, a great kid with a big fish, and a smoky tequila accompanied by the sound of loons. Now the same island was occupied by a family of campers. We paddled back down the lake and chose a much less attractive campsite, that became even worse when we discovered the first litter of our trip: cigarette butts, foil, discarded food. Bummer. We knew we were getting closer to civilization.

We fished hard after supper and the fish bit harder. It was the best fishing of the trip, with lots of action. There was no breeze that night and we slept on top of our sleeping bags, sweating in the dark.

Day 6

We awoke early and fished before breakfast. Tom caught a lunker smallmouth and later snagged his best lure on the bottom. We paddled to shore, he stripped, putting his clothes on a flat rock, and he followed the line out, hand over hand, diving deep to retrieve his lure. He came up, shaking his head like a dog. He swam ashore, and as he stood on the rock naked, reeling in his free line, I snapped his picture. He turned away at the last instant, relieving the photo lab of any difficult decisions. I told him I was putting the picture on a T-shirt labeled, "Fish naked!"

As we ate pancakes for breakfast, the breeze kicked up. Frothy whitecaps began licking at the beach and the canoe rocked back and forth, half in and half out of the water. We filleted the fish for later, and packed up our gear. For the first time, we lashed everything in the boat and put on our life jackets rather than using them as seat cushions. Crossing Phoebe was interesting. The strong wind held the canoe so that despite both of us paddling on the right side, we didn't swing to the left. The wind blew water into my face, keeping my sunglasses wet, and the world a misty blur.

We made Grace Lake, and were dismayed to see large whitecaps wrinkling the lake like pewter corduroy. The surf pushed us to a sheltered cove where we waited until the wind calmed, finally creeping along the shoreline to the portage. The trail was the worse since Day 1. It was a one-hundred sixty rod boulder field. I went ahead with the food pack on the second leg, thinking I would drop it and return to help Tom with the canoe.

I reached the lake and slid out of the pack, did a couple of toe touches to stretch, and turned around to start back up the trail. He was already coming around the last bend. "Piece of cake," was all he said.

Lake Ella was the smallest of the sisters, and I think the prettiest. She was long and slim. Dan and I had caught wall-hangers there nine-years ago. Tom and I were alone on the lake. We had a great campsite, the same one Dan and I enjoyed before. It had smooth flat rocks, and was breezy with no bugs. We had two hours to kill before supper. We set up camp and lay in the sun in the exact place where I had caught the big northern that now is swimming on the wall over my fireplace. I remembered Dan watching his Dad like no one but a nine year old can. I dozed in and out. It was too breezy to fish anyway.

I took a walk before supper and found two beaver-stripped sticks to take home, reminding me of father and son and fulfilling a promise. We pan-fried walleye steaks that night and had the last of our bourbon and lemonade. Boundary Sours, we call them. And, we had the last of our cigars. Before turning in, we built a crackling fire and watched the sparks drift up, blending with the stars.

Day 7

We loaded and portaged twice, meeting a family coming from Beth Lake, four healthy kids and outdoorsy parents. The Dad had an old Colonel Potter campaign hat, like one that I sometimes wear and for which I am unmercifully chided. "See?" I thought. The youngest daughter was wearing a gigantic Duluth pack stuffed with sleeping bags on her back, and from behind she looked like a pack with feet. Tom took a picture. We talked with her mother about this year's blueberry crop and the blackberry seeds in the bear droppings deposited in the middle of the portage trail. She spoke of a problem bear around Beth Lake like we talk about nuisance potholes on Main Street.

We pack-muled on to Alton Lake and filtered more water. We had long since used all of our paper filters and we were washing out the remaining filter with the last few cups in our water jug. It's a wonder we didn't catch beaver fever.

We were down to the last portage trail...and we couldn't find it, at least for a while. Finally, there it was, hidden in a tiny cove. It was an easy thirty rods back to Sawbill Lake. As we paddled south toward the base, we passed grandmas and kids and day-tourists in rented canoes. Tom and I had grown beards and we were sun-brown. My shirt was torn and I knew my wife would demand that my filthy khaki pants be burned. We were Lewis and Clark, or Himalayan climbers. We had been to the Mountain.

As we beached our canoe and unloaded, a fraternity group walked down to the lake accompanied by a Sawbill guide. One of the young men asked me where we had been. "Louse River," I replied. The guide looked at us admiringly and said, "Cool!" like youngsters do nowadays. The frats looked at us, not as two guys who could have been their fathers, but as two adventurers.

As I walked toward the Sawbill Store for a shower, Tom took my picture. It felt odd, standing in front of a store with people and cars and not ebbing in the sparkling lake with the sun and breeze in my face. Later I took a shower and watched the last of the Boundary Waters run off my legs, swirling into the drain. Tom bought me an ice cold beer, a local brew called Pig's Eye Ale. I hoped and imagined they used Boundary Waters like Coors uses Rockies spring water. Regardless, it was cold and delicious.

After

On my desk at work is a foot-long willow branch, stripped clean with serrations made by the teeth of a beaver. I run my hand over the patterned wood and feel the portage rocks, taste the water, and hear a loon. In my fishing hat at home is a big brown feather I picked up on one of the Sisters.

I suppose it could be an eagle's, but it doesn't matter. The mere
fact that it could have been dropped by the eagle at Mesaba brings
back the blue of the sky, the smell of a campfire, the look on
Tom's face when the pike took the sunfish. I smile.

Sometimes when I'm driving on a winding road, I want to dig my
paddle in on the left to turn, twisting my wrist to jay its blade as I
feel the waves and current. Foraying boundaries will do that. It is
comforting to know that I can return there in my dreams, and,
when the time is right, in reality. It is still there.

Photo by Randy Waterhouse

North Woods Sky and Water

CHAPTER 8

MISTAKEN IDENTITY

I enjoy "freestyle" bowhunting. Several years ago I grew weary of being tethered to specific stand locations and lock-on stands over food plots, funnels, and the like, and I purchased a high quality lightweight climbing tree stand. There's a certain comfort in knowing exactly where you will be hunting on a given afternoon and being able to sneak in and climb right up in your stand. But the freedom to wander the woods searching for hot locations and being able to climb just about any tree based on wind direction and the fickle habits of whitetail deer is very attractive to me. I also do not use trail cameras. I'm somewhat electronically challenged, but the main reason is that I like surprises. Knowing exactly which deer will appear at what time would take away some of the fun of the hunt, the enjoyment of the chess match.

One of my most memorable hunts involved a surprise. It was a beautiful late autumn afternoon. I hiked into a remote corner of my favorite public hunting area and waded a river only to find that none of the white oak trees that had been traditional deer magnets were dropping acorns.

I stood scratching my head and gazing at the nearby bluffs, looking for a spot to salvage my afternoon hunt, when I glimpsed a small seam in the topography on the bluff about three hundred yards up-slope from my position.

"Maybe there's a trail up there," I mused.

I cinched my backpack, shouldered my tree stand and climbed the steep slope. Sure enough, there was a narrow terrace, a well-worn deer trail, and a big white oak that was dropping acorns. The ground had been scuffed up by deer and turkeys, and there was a tall straight poplar tree perfectly located to serve as an ambush tree. I hung a scent wick fifteen yards in front of me, strapped my stand on the poplar's trunk and shimmied up to a good vantage point to watch the afternoon's performance.

An hour before dark, a buck noisily chased a doe down the trail, and despite the sexiest bleats I could muster, I couldn't get him to stop for a shot. A half hour before dusk I heard a deer walking in the river bottom below me, and with every other step I could hear a distinctive "uurp." It sounded like a mature buck.

I picked up my can call and bleated. The deer stopped. I bleated again, and here he came, like he was on a string. Every time he "uurped" I bleated. I slowly stood up and made ready to shoot. The buck came closer and closer. Finally, "he" popped out of the honeysuckle. I was astonished to see that "he" was a big doe. She grunted once more and walked to the scent wick. She turned broadside and I shot her. The shot looked good, and I thought I heard her crash in the brush. I gathered up my gear and started down the tree. Then I heard a deer snort from the direction my deer had run. Rather than risk bumping a wounded deer, I quietly descended the tree, hiked back down the slope and waded the river in the dark. The rocks were slippery and my flashlight reflected off of the black water, hiding its depth. I used my bow as a walking stick to avoid an unwanted swim. The long hike back to my truck was eerie.

I was re-playing the shot in my head while watching the surrounding forest for those night creatures that lurk just behind the knowledge that nothing out there will grab me.

The temperature was already starting to drop and I could see my breath. I knew that the deer wouldn't spoil if I found it early enough in the morning. The sun's rays were just peeking over the horizon as I waded back across the river.

I climbed the bluff, carrying a canvas internal frame pack that I have used to haul big game quarters for a quarter century. Except for four nylon game bags, a meat saw, knives, and a knife sharpener, it was empty. I hoped it would be full on the return hike. I topped the slope and walked straight to my scent wick. Just beyond it I found my broken arrow, matted slick with dried blood. I walked in the direction of the deer's crash and found the doe fifty yards further, piled up against a big tree. The snort I heard must have come from another deer. I quartered her and put the quarters in the game bags and into my pack. The meat was still warm but smelled sweet. I hurried, gathering my gear, pulling on my pack and picking my way down the slope, tacking from to tree to tree, hanging on to low limbs to give me stability. I reached the bottom and scurried across a hundred yards of forest to the river. I quickly slipped out of my pack, unloaded it, and lowered the bags into the cold stream. I tied them to a big log, and they slowly moved in the current like a raft of decoys. I sat down on a log, knowing that it wouldn't take long for the meat to chill.

Meat bags cooling in the river.

The mist was just burning off of the river. The underbrush along the shore and the river birch were brownish pewter. The hardwoods on the surrounding hills looked like woodsmoke, a misty grey. The air was cool and smelled like fresh cut hickory and damp earth. This little valley is isolated from the adjacent farmland by the topography, and I felt like I was in Alaska or a mountain wilderness. I listened, and the only sound was the rustle of brown leaves in the breeze, water running over river stones, and a distant crow.

I thought about how the doe had completely surprised me. I had several doe tags, and I love venison. I pondered whether a buck would have made this a better hunt. No, I don't think so. This was really an exceptional hunt. The surprise made the hunt more enjoyable.

As I sat there on that log, smoking the cigar I save for special occasions, I thought to myself, "This hunt was way too cool!" I'm in my mid-sixties, but I sometimes think and act like a kid, probably the result of being around my three children, who are now in their thirties. Sometimes I regress and say Cool or Dude. So, I thought again, "This hunt was way too cool!" I even said it out loud. Things don't always go as planned.

As hunters, particularly those who compromise our chances to kill animals by using traditional equipment, we almost expect to go home and eat tag soup. But it sure is nice to have a game plan that actually works. To enjoy a pleasant surprise is a bonus, icing on the cake.

What is a "good" hunt? I took an outdoor recreation class when I was in college. One of the interesting things I learned was how to objectively evaluate outdoor recreation experiences. The criteria I have developed for my personal hunting adventures are: remote environment, landscape beauty, challenge, wildlife encounters, and having the opportunity to achieve my harvest goals. This hunt was nearly perfect….a nine and there are very few tens.

I lifted the dripping game bags from the stream and hung them from a limb to drain and chill in the breeze. I sat back down and re-lit my cigar. This was one of those celebrations I look forward to. I was in a beautiful place, an isolated location, with a challenging hike, and a deer in the backpack. Despite the deer's mistaken identity, the hunt was memorable. Cool!

Author's note: This story first appeared in the March 2015 **Traditional Bowhunter (Online) Magazine**.

The deer that fooled me.

CHAPTER 9

LONE STAR JAVELINA

I looked across the riot of spring color and listened to the sounds of unfamiliar birds from my perch on a tripod stand over a windmill-fed waterhole. I was just thirty miles north of Mexico in South Texas and I smiled at my luck.

This was one of those "a friend of a friend" deals that we sometimes fall into. My buddy, John, was a wrangler and hunting guide on this 40,000 acre (small by Texas standards) section of the fabled King Ranch over thirty years ago and he still exchanges Christmas cards with the manager. When John asked me if I might like to try and arrow a javelina during the off-season when the lodge was empty, I jumped at the chance. We met Mark, a South Carolina Hall of Fame high school basketball coach, in Nashville, and hit the road. John and Mark are avid turkey hunters, and the chance to bag a Rio Grande longbeard was the primary attraction for them.

Over the years, I've arrowed a turkey or two, but that endeavor always seems to coincide with the spring white bass run in my favorite Bluegrass streams, and the allure of dropping a Marabou Muddler into a cold clear eddy after letting my favorite 4-weight rod hibernate for several months is irresistible, so turkeys have always played second fiddle. But javelina, on the other hand, are critters of a different color. Experiencing the sights and sounds of South Texas, eating some authentic Tex-Mex food, and arrowing an animal indigenous to that locale would be a real treat.

Back to the waterhole. It was a breezy afternoon, cool for South Texas. The sound of songbirds was a symphony and I tried to decipher the identities of the musicians.

The Grackles were the loudest, and I could easily spot their black forms flying in and out of the low trees. I finally pinpointed the Green Jays and their tunes. Green Jays have a blue head, green body, and a yellow tail, and are about the same size as their blue northern cousins. I spotted a Mexican Eagle soaring on the breeze looking for a snack, maybe a lizard or a rattlesnake. He was low enough that I could see his orange crest. Across the waterhole along the brush line I caught movement. I lifted my binoculars and identified a Roadrunner, another newcomer to my repertoire of bird knowledge. Man, was I having fun! Just being there was awesome.

A shadow moved through the mesquite thicket. I brought my bow up and eased to my feet. One shadow became two and then three. Soon a sounder of javelina emerged on a sandy trail and trotted toward the water. The largest of the group paused broadside. It was a chip shot. I drew my bow, anchored and released. And I missed. The whole herd scattered. I sat down and shook my head. How in the world could I have missed such an easy shot? I had fallen victim to the malady that afflicts all traditional bowhunters from time to time. In my excitement I had failed to pick a spot. And, predictably, I missed.

Javelina are distant cousins to pigs, sharing a common ancestor millions of years ago. The correct name for javelina is Collared Peccary, an apt description due to the band of whitish fir around their necks. They range across the American southwest, and are common in south Texas, southern Arizona, and southern New Mexico. They are primarily herbivores, and eat prickly pear cactus, mesquite beans, live oak acorns, tubers and roots. A large male will weigh around sixty pounds. Javelina have a scent gland on their lower backs, giving them a perhaps erroneous nickname, "skunk pigs." They have a great sense of smell, but poor eyesight, making them perfect for a traditional or primitive archer.

It wasn't long until the birds returned. The sun's rays touched the horizon and I knew that this beautiful day would soon conclude. A coyote yelped a quarter mile away, and was followed by another from a slightly different direction.

When I learned I would be making this hunting trip, I contacted my buddy Steven Rinella of Meateater TV. We had shared a campfire on an elk hunt and still talk from time to time. Steve had told me about a magic javelina call that he had used with great success. Steve warned me to wear thick trousers, as javelina have been known to respond to the call by charging the hunter and literally climbing up his leg. So, I bought one and practiced, much to my wife's chagrin. The call sounds a lot like your standard run-of-the-mill distressed rabbit predator call. When I heard the two coyotes yipping, I pulled the call from my pocket and gave it a few wails. I stood up and knocked an arrow.

Less than a minute later two coyotes emerged from the woods to my right, no more than fifteen yards away. The problem was a big tree limb that blocked any chance of a shot. Whoever erected the tripod stand had done an admirable job in nestling it against a mesquite tree for camouflage, but a big limb blocked any chance of a shot in just that direction. The coyotes seemed intent on the croaking of the frogs in the waterhole, which allowed me to softly shuffle my body around to give me a chance at a shot if they cleared the end of the limb. But they didn't. I enjoyed seeing the two critters up close and personal. The evening breeze blew their amber fur, and their noses searched the air for the scent of that distressed rabbit. They finally lost interest and faded back into the brush. The sun dropped and the day was over.

The next morning found me in another tripod stand, nestled against another mesquite tree at the edge of a clearing containing an old rusty corn feeder that is used during the whitetail deer season. It was empty and currently non-functioning. Some of the local cowboys had seen a group of javelina in the area the day before, and the clearing was pock-marked by tiny tracks.

The prickly pear cactus were blooming bright yellow bouquets and many of their paddle-shaped leaves were serrated with little oval cutouts from the sharp teeth of javelina. I hoped they would return to dine on the succulent cactus leaves.

It was another beautiful day. I was entertained by the birds, and even the bugs. Cattle had moved through the area and had deposited their trademark cow pies. Around each pile, the industrious dung beetles had landed and were busy rolling up little balls of manure. Several piles were directly below my stand, and I was able to focus on the beetles with my binoculars. Hunting in South Texas is not boring.

Javelina finally did appear, and this time I remembered to pick a spot. My arrow hit one of the larger pigs perfectly. It grunted and sped off into a grove or "mot" of live oaks. I saw it emerge on the far side and enter a thicket of mesquite. Then all was quiet.

I turned my attention back to the sounder. Most of the group had fled, but one grizzled pig paused and walked across an opening. I took a shot, and my arrow nicked a branch. It hit the animal through the back quarters, and it scurried into a nearby thicket.

I knew that the shot on the first pig had been lethal, so I focused on the wounded javelina. I quickly climbed down from my perch and circled the thicket to get the wind in my face. I spotted the critter, who also spotted me. It began chattering its teeth as a warning. I took two steps to the right to gain an opening to its vitals, and I anchored it for good.

It only took a few minutes to locate the first one I had shot and I carried both of the pigs to a shady spot near my tripod stand. I climbed back up into my perch to continue watching the Texas wildlife show.

Javies are toothy critters.

Less than a half hour later, I was sitting there watching the largest whitetail buck I have ever seen. It had emerged from the far tree line and stood twenty yards away feeding on tender spring grass.

I thumbed my bowstring, yearning for the chance to send an arrow toward this once-in-a-lifetime deer. But, alas, deer season was just a memory, and this old bruiser would be dropping his headgear any day now to begin life's cycle of renewal. Oh well.

It had been a productive hunt. My buddy, John, and my new friend Mark had both shotgunned fat longbeards. Mark had shot an old hump-backed wild hog with his rifle, and John had also killed a javelina with his compound bow.

I was with him when he shot it and I still laugh when I remember his silent celebratory "Javie dance." He's a great guy and a hoot to share a hunting camp with.

Javelinas' reputation as stinky nasty animals is unfounded. Both of the animals I shot were females, and didn't stink at all. I was careful around the scent glands when skinning them, but no other precautions were necessary. Small Texas towns are charming and friendly. I collect "mantiques" and just about every town has at least one antique shop. Many of the little business districts have an old-time saloon with good local food.

Texas, as we all have read, has limited public land hunting opportunities, but there are a few. Go to the Texas Parks and Wildlife website to check out opportunities. South Texas has a year-round javelina season with a bag limit of two. North Texas javie hunting is limited to winter months. Arizona has a spring and fall season and tags are offered through a state tag drawing. Go to the Arizona Fish and Game website for application information. New Mexico javelina hunting is also an application drawing hunt. Go to the New Mexico Department of Fish and Game website for info. Guides and outfitters operate in all three states and a website search will list several. You may be able to arrange a "drop camp" deal with an outfitter for a modest fee, that will give you some land access, but allow you to hunt on your own. Generally, if you can find a private land opportunity in Texas, that will be your best opportunity for success. For all hunts, make sure to check the current seasons, license requirements, and hunting regulations

When I return from a hunting trip, I always do a hunt critique, trying to come up with things I might do differently upon my return. If I ever get a chance to do another Texas javie hunt I would definitely try some spot-and-stalk javelina hunting. However, live oak trees drop their old leaves in the spring, carpeting the ground with a potato chip-like noisy layer, so a still-hunter would have to avoid live oak mots.

But hunting slowly from sendero (two-track) to sendero into the wind would be fun. I would also try to arrow a Rio Grande turkey.

On this trip I tried my Rinella-endorsed javelina call several times with no luck. In all fairness to Steve, on the days I tried the call, it was extremely windy. When I reported this back to Steve after the hunt he said I must have blown into the wrong end of the call. You know, maybe he was right!

Author's note: This story first appeared in the January 2018 issue of **Primitive Archer** magazine.

A mature javelina will weigh around sixty pounds.

Recipe- Javelina meat is similar in texture and color to feral hog meat. I wanted my culinary efforts to be in keeping with where I killed these critters, so I focused on Tex-Mex cuisine. Here's a recipe for javelina fajitas I pulled from the TPWD website, and I modified it a bit.

2-3 pound javelina ham, bone-in.

Salt and pepper to taste

2 packages of chili seasoning mix.

1 TBS brown sugar

1 TBS ground cumin

1 TBS oregano

2 onions chopped

1 green pepper chopped

1 cup water

1-2 TBS olive oil.

A dozen soft tortilla shells browned in a skillet in vegetable oil

Guacamole

Your favorite salsa

At least one ice-cold beer per person.

Preheat your oven to 225-250 . Season javelina ham with salt, pepper, cumin, chili seasoning, sugar, and oregano by rubbing the entire ham. Add just enough olive oil to cover the bottom of a large skillet or small Dutch oven. Brown the ham on the stove. Place the onions and peppers on the bottom, lay the ham on the onions and peppers, add the water, cover the pan with a tight lid, and bake for four hours. Remove the ham, slice the meat thinly or "pull" it, and serve everything on tortillas with salsa and /or guacamole. And don't forget to give each guest a beer!

CHAPTER 10

A BAD DAY FISHING

They say that there are no bad days fishing. Normally I agree, but this one had been bad.

From time to time I will donate a guided fly fishing trip to a local charity to auction at a fund raising event. That is why I was standing, net in hand, behind a fisherman in one of my favorite boulder-strewn pools in my favorite stream. He had just caught a fifteen inch smallmouth, and the weather that day was what makes October in Kentucky the best season of the year.

My phone, which I keep sealed in a Ziploc bag in my pack when wading, rang. I usually keep it turned off when I'm in the woods, but I forgot to do so. I was a bit shocked that I actually had service in this remote area. I turned and waded ashore and fished it out of my pack. I had missed the call so I hit the call back button. The familiar voice of a friend who lives in the mountains of Eastern Kentucky answered.

"Really glad to hear your voice!" he said emphatically.

"Why? What's up?", I asked.

He replied, "I just got a call from the local conservation officer. He told me that an Elk Foundation employee has been shot. I thought it was you."

So began, for me, a nightmare that had started with me standing in a stream on a beautiful day, and ended with me delivering a eulogy at Eric Crook's memorial service.

Eric had called me that morning as I drove to meet my angler. A couple of weeks earlier Eric had asked me to assist him in guiding an Indiana elk hunter who had drawn a coveted Kentucky elk tag. I had to decline due my scheduled fishing trip, but I told him to call if he needed anything. And that morning, he did. He and his hunter were sitting on a ridge glassing for elk, and hadn't seen one all morning. He asked if I had any suggestions. I mentioned a couple of good spots and gave him the number of another friend who is an outstanding elk guide. The last thing Eric said to me was, "Thanks, good buddy."

Eric was the real deal. He was an experienced outdoorsman, accomplished Alaskan guide, and an exceptional hunter and woodsman. He usually carried a .454 Casul western-style revolver in a custom made leather holster on his hip when in the woods. It had a thong that looped over the hammer of the gun to keep it in the holster. Over the years he had drawn his gun several times when encountering inland grizzly bears, critters that are more ill-tempered that their coastal cousins. It was a gun Eric had carried a long time, and one with which he was comfortable.

This particular revolver did not have a transfer bar, a little metal plate that sits between the un-cocked hammer and the rear of the bullet to keep the gun from firing should the back of the hammer be struck. On one occasion, while sitting around a campfire, we had discussed the efficacy of not keeping a live round under the hammer of a revolver.

But, on that fateful day, when Eric bent over to retrieve a soft drink from a cooler, the leather thong had slipped off. There was a live round under the hammer, and when the gun fell out of the holster, it hit the bed of his truck, discharged, and fatally wounded my good friend.

Eric lived for over an hour, enduring a bumpy ride in the bed of his truck and a helicopter flight to a hospital. He died shortly after arriving in the ER, leaving his grieving widow, Karen, and shocked friends.

Eric had been an exceptional camp cook. On one occasion in our Kentucky elk camp, Eric concocted a dessert by heating a mixture of frozen strawberries, raspberries, and blueberries, mixed with several of his secret adult beverages. He lit the whole thing on fire, and poured it over frozen Klondike Bars.

When we tasted it, one of the hunters in our group exclaimed, "This is better than sex!" With a twinkle in his eye, Eric looked at Karen and said, "I guess it depends on who you are with." That got a good laugh.

After Eric's passing, the dust settled and we all returned to our lives. Except Karen. She still wakes up every day missing her husband and best friend. Many of us now try to live our lives a little better to honor Eric's memory.

Fall turned into winter, winter to spring, and finally the long bright days of summer arrived. When mid-October rolled around, I had a nagging dread. I had not fished the river in a year, but maybe, I thought, the cold clear water and the sound of the river tumbling over the rocks would ease the gloom.

So, I gathered up my gear, borrowed a soft cooler, and drove the thirty miles to the river. I fished upstream for several hours to the boulder pool, where I sat down on a ledge and fired up my backpacking stove. Thinking about my friend, I stirred the steaming berry syrup and ladled it over a Klondike Bar. I held a spoonful up to the blue sky and said, "Here's to you Good Buddy."

Photo by Karen Crook

Eric Crook

CHAPTER 11

WINTER RESPITE

In the stone grey of winter, after the mid-January closing of the deer archery season, I let my arm rest. Oh, I may give a try at half-heartedly calling coyotes on a sunny day in February, but mainly I catalog my equipment, catch up on my journals, sharpen arrows, and dream about the promise of deer I saw but didn't harvest. And, I let my arm rest.

From the spring turkey season on through an occasional foray into the Canadian bear woods, and into and through autumn, I shoot my little recurve every single day. Most of the deer I've killed were done so in the fog of pure instinct. I know I attempted to pick a spot, (there's a message written on the upper limb of my bow that says, "Pick a spot!") and focus on that spot until I release an arrow, but at the pivotal moment when I decide to shoot, more often than not, pure instinct takes over and my muscle memory repeats what has happened a million times since spring. Frankly, when I see antlers bobbing through the trees it's hard for me to keep my wits about me enough to do much more than that, and through sheer repetition, I know that with or without my wits, my arm probably won't fail me.

Every morning I get up at 5:30, go for a jog, eat, shower, dress for work, and then in the half-light of dawn I shoot my bow for a few minutes. Because I shoot instinctively, if I can make out the target, I can shoot...and I certainly don't need enough light to peer through a peep sight.

Then in the evenings I'll poke around behind the house, tossing a foam ball and firing off blunts or judos at varying distances. But, day after day of flinging arrows tires my arm and my mind. So, in the winter, I let it rest.

This weekend I think I'll feed the critters. Biologists tell me it's a bad idea, but occasionally in the depths of cabin-fever season, I'll take a fifty pound bag of cracked corn to my favorite woodlot and leave corn strewn about. It probably offers no more than a single meal to the tribes of whitetails and squirrels and turkeys, but I like to think it keeps them hanging around. Of course, I can't do that just before and during turkey season, as corn is illegal and the Achilles heel for turkeys. I'd like to carry my bow, even though I haven't drawn it for a month and my arm is still hibernating, as I can't imagine being in the woods without my old friend, but I think I'll leave it at home, and let it rest too.

This is also the season of dream hunts. I plan hunts that feature, more than any other element, freedom. I have honed my equipment over the last decade, first by pounds and now by ounces. I can mentally calculate the weight of the gear I'll need for a seven day backpack hunt for elk. Savings in weight means mobility (and thus freedom), an attribute that is mandatory in pursuit of elk in the vast wildernesses of our western forests. In my dreams I plan my gear, my itinerary, my strategy, and I mentally run my fingers over maps of wilderness areas, hoping to feel the ridges and streams. I hold those dreams until they materialize in the frosty September meadows of Colorado or New Mexico.

New adventures sometimes come from these dreams. I made a mental note last June to explore a tilted ravine that bisects the cliffs lining my favorite Kentucky wilderness trout stream. The mental note may become an analysis of a topo map, an exploratory insertion to scout for deer sign, and maybe a full-blown back-pack adventure next fall. Or maybe not. After all, it's late winter, and I'm dreaming.

I sometimes dream about the perfect hunt, that mythical occasion when it all comes together...the wild place, the adventure of it all, the companionship, the animals. Of all of my hunts in wonderful places...the misty Canadian wilds, the deep green Florida swamps, the vermillion mesas of New Mexico and Utah, the wildernesses of Colorado, and the breathtaking colors of Kentucky autumns, I can label only one hunt as "perfect." It was truly an adventure.

In 1991, it had been more than a decade since I finished graduate school and departed the mountain west for my home in Kentucky. But, the lure of the mountains tugged at me constantly. Sometimes, when driving on our rural roads, and the clouds were just so, I would peer up through my windshield and my imagination would see the Bear River Mountains to my east, mirages from my memory. And the big antlered mule deer hanging in my den reminded me daily of the mountains I had grown to love and miss.

So, my fellow adventurer, Tom, and I planned a hunt. We compared information on various states: the size of the elk herds, success statistics, accessibility, the chances of getting drawn for a tag, the cost, the distance. Once a week we would spread maps out on the kitchen table and imagine ourselves crossing the prairies toward distant mountains. We poured over trip lists and menus of freeze-dried faire. We ran and lifted weights daily. When we left Kentucky on Labor Day weekend we were loaded like hillbillies. The first day of September found us camped by a crystal clear stream four miles into the San Pedro Parks Wilderness in northern New Mexico.

We hunted hard, walking a dozen miles a day. On Monday I saw a bear. On Tuesday I saw a whopper mule deer just out of range. On Wednesday I arrowed a fat cow elk. And on Thursday night, Tom got lost. Bad lost. At dark, he simply misjudged where camp was and walked off of the wrong side of a ridge. I stayed up late poking the fire and calling out his name whenever I heard a twig snap in the dark or a glop of frozen rain hitting the tarp.

I looked for him at dawn for several hours with no luck, and I finally left a note in camp telling him I was going for help. I hiked out and went to town to round up a search and rescue. Meanwhile, Tom hiked out to a road and flagged down a ranger, who radioed the office. When I finally picked him up, he looked like hell and smelled like it, literally. Seems he'd spent the night curled up around a pitiful fire. His face was sooty and his eyes hollow. He'd walked at least ten miles that morning on an empty stomach. I felt like kissing him. I gave him a beer instead. Tom is a beer expert.

For his fiftieth birthday I gave him a handmade wooden trout net. In a very utilitarian way he said he really appreciated it and would use it a lot. Another friend gave him fifty beers of different brands and countries of origin. Tom cried. Tears of joy rained on Glenwood Springs Pale Ales and Itchy Dog Lagers.

So, when I picked him up after his night lost in the mountains, I gave him a beer. It was lukewarm and was one of those twelve-packs for five bucks brands. He'd normally bitch and turn up his nose in a good natured way. This time he gulped it down without talking or breathing.

We hiked back to camp, packed up, and hauled our gear back to the car. (Luckily we'd packed the quartered elk out on Thursday morning.) We drove out the north end of the wilderness through a small town called Coyote, looking for a place to eat. The only place there was a double-wide with a beer sign. So, we drove east, and suddenly, like some sort of Twilight Zone experience, we came upon a restaurant with ferns and sitar music and sunflower seed salads in a town called Abiquiu. Our buxom waitress was a twenty year old with a lacy dress and, as I recall, a red dot between her eyes. She said her cowboy husband was out elk hunting. We left Abiquiu, full and rubbing our stomachs. Our systems were a bit shocked after a week of granola.

We drove east toward Santa Fe. Suddenly the traffic backed up.
Probably a football game, I thought. I looked at Tom and he was
snoring. I rolled down the window and asked a traffic cop who was
playing. He said the Santa Fe Opera. No way! Yes way.

We made eastern New Mexico, a place called Las Vegas I believe,
by dark. Not to be confused with the Las Vegas in Nevada, this
place had only one "resort" hotel, a small Motel 6, and it had
plenty of vacancies. I tried to wake Tom but couldn't. He just
wouldn't wake up. (If you're ever struck with insomnia, hike ten
miles on an empty stomach after sleeping on rocks in the rain
curled up around a campfire, and then drink a beer and eat a big
meal.) I went into the room and took a shower. My guilty
conscience got the best of me and I went out to the car to either
wake him or throw a sleeping bag over his dead body. He sat up
and said what and where and I led him into the room and to bed
like a blind man.

The next day we drove northeast across western Kansas. I thought
about turning north to see the site of Black Kettle's Sand Creek
massacre, but I'd seen Wounded Knee a few years earlier, and
once you see one tragic chapter in our history, you've seen them
all. We did go through Dodge City and just east of that sleepy little
town we came upon a sign that said, "Scenic View Ahead."
Shortly we wound our way up a hill and there was a pull off. We
turned in. A historic marker stood next to a set of those big look-
in-the-binoculars-for-fifty-cents contraptions. Below us a gigantic
cloud of dust was being raised by probably five hundred acres of
cattle standing flank to flank, nose to tail. I'm talking thousands,
no, millions of them. We both said, okaaay, and drove on.

We made Kentucky two days later. Even after munching on
French fries all the way back, Tom had still lost ten pounds, but we
were a hundred pounds richer in memories. The perfect hunt.

You know bowhunting is not merely something you do, when you find yourself looking at next year's calendar within the framework of nature's cycles rather than fiscal years.

If the whitetail rut goes into your day-planner before birthdays and tax deadlines, you're there. It's who you are. The notation, "Rest Arm" that is penciled in on the third week in January signals the annual washing of camo, greasing broadheads, and catching up on journals as I watch the wet snow pile up on the two yellow haybales stacked neatly exactly twenty five yards from my back porch.

Sometimes I fish in the winter. My favorite trout stream is no wider than a city street and tumbles out of the Daniel Boone National Forest. The dead of winter in Kentucky can mean zero degrees or sixty degrees. If you don't like the weather, wait a minute. The water is gin-clear and flows over a sandy rock bottom through boulder fields and rhododendron thickets. Warm winter days melt the fringe ice and send beams of sunlight through the pewter trees, warming the water, and waking the aquatic insects and predatory trout from a winter slumber. I tie on tiny nymphs and let them drift into blue-green pools. Sometimes I'll slowly work a streamer through pocket-water, and when I hook a fish the rod throbs like a slender wand and I net the red-shouldered trout. Sometimes I release them, always the larger ones, but often I kill a few for supper. My bent fly rod has become the arc that I substitute for the arc of my bow. If I am living well, the rod sends the line and the fly perfectly, without a splash, like my bow sends the arrow, a gleaming bird, perfectly, replaying months of repetition and a winter of rest.

It's now early March. The snow is off the bales and the redbuds are swelling. The beginnings of the green narcissus shoots are fingering out at the edge of the woodpile. My arm still throbs, but not with the ache of a long autumn, but with the anticipation of full-draws and dream seasons to be.

If I'm living well, the rod sends the fly perfectly.

CHAPTER 12

SHIVAKI

This fall, I developed more than a passing interest in bear turds. As a Kentucky elk guide, I was struck by the abundance of bear scat. The autumn olive trees had a bumper crop of red berries, and bears love them. At least a quarter of the autumn olives I saw had been destroyed by bears climbing up into the middle of the foliage and literally jumping up and down to pull the limbs close enough to the ground to reach the berries. The resulting bear turds were brownish pink and choc-full of semi-digested berries.

This year's woods also had an abundance of acorns. There were some wooded ridges that had been roto-tilled by marauding bears looking for acorns, and monstrous piles of droppings were scattered about. One particular elongated yellowish turd I found was as big around as my wrist. Usually a big rear-end means a big bear.

So, on opening day, I was standing, camouflaged, in an autumn olive thicket, next to a camouflaged bowhunter and tooting a call meant to sound like a young sexy cow elk. That made me a little nervous. When I saw what I thought was a black angus beef cow weaving through the underbrush toward us, my mental bear alarm should have sounded. The four hundred pound bruin was only fifteen feet away when my right hand flipped the leather thong off the hammer of my.44 magnum and I hollered "Hey bear!" The bear was as shocked as I was and he immediately galloped away.

I looked at my hunter and said nervously, "That was cool." He replied, "That *was* cool." I then *really* started paying attention to the bear turds.

No other close encounters resulted, but at the time of this writing I still have one bowhunter who, after passing up several bulls, hopes to achieve a last minute Hail Mary the last day of the season. I guess the jury is still out regarding whether my bones will end up in a bear turd this year.

Scat, is a polite term for shit. My hunting buddy, John, who doesn't cuss much, calls it shivaki. Scat has always fascinated me. As a young bowhunter, I had a scat collection. I would put droppings in the sun to dry for a few days, varnish them to make them look shiny fresh, and I would store them in meticulously labeled plastic 35mm film canisters. (For those of you youngsters who don't know what a film canister is, look it up in an encyclopedia. What's an encyclopedia? ...never mind. Google it.) I finally lost interest and pitched my scat collection. I eventually figured out that if I wanted to preserve scat it's a lot more practical to take a photo of it and label the photo. For instance: "9/12/97 Moose- Boulder Mountain, Utah". Finally I lost interest in even that and now I only take scat pictures from time to time on my cell phone for the occasional seminar power point.

At one point in my bowhunting "career", I taught Bowhunter Education classes. Before the field portion of each class where I would discuss tree stand safety, blood trailing, and reading sign, I would slip out to the woods and scatter little piles of raisins. During the class session I would pick up a raisin, sniff it, hold it up to the light and say something like, "two and a half year old doe that is blind in one eye." Then I would pop the raisin into my mouth, chew it, and say, "blind in the left eye." Woods humor.

I do enjoy examining scat. For one thing, you really can cipher that an animal had actually been there, in that exact spot. To some degree you can guess how long ago the scat was deposited, whether the animal was standing or walking, how big it was, and with a little poking or prodding, what the animal had been eating. Anything beyond that is pure speculation and borders on sorcery.

Let's distill a typical scenario. You find several piles of elk scat in the timber. Some have pellets the size of black olives, some the size of green olives, and some the size of peas. They are all shiny and have gnats and flies on them. Scattered about are three foot by six foot oval depressions in the foliage. What does this tell us? I would guess that a small herd of elk bedded here within the last twenty four hours, and that the herd consisted of at least one calf, one cow, and one bull. Conclusion: This might be a good morning set-up to catch the elk coming back from their feeding grounds to bed. This, of course, is pure speculation, based on interpreting the sign. Who really knows the mind of an elk?

Raccoon scat is interesting and a good indicator of what's happening in the woods. Raccoons are omnivorous and are opportunistic feeders. Finding a coon turd full of persimmon seeds means there is a persimmon tree nearby that is dropping ripe fruit. Finding that tree is a pretty good strategy for hanging a tree stand nearby to intercept a whitetail. A raccoon turd containing crayfish shells may indicate that the nearby stream would be a good place to cast a Nearnuff Crayfish fly for fat smallmouth bass. Raccoon droppings containing blackberry seeds means it is time to come back with a bucket to collect the main ingredient for blackberry cobbler.

Believe it or not, there is a scientific discipline dedicated to studying dinosaur scat. Really? Petrified dinosaur turds are called coprolites and their contents can reveal what sort of small vegetarian dinosaur a T-Rex had for lunch. I actually found a coprolite when I was a kid and I kept it in a shoebox full of arrowheads, sea shells, and buckeyes.

My collection became the victim of adolescence and is lost. I sure wish I still had that coprolite. Most animals simply defecate when and where they happen to be when the urge strikes them. However, a few species always deposit droppings in the same spot. I was recently on a javelina hunt in south Texas and happened upon large heaps of elk-like droppings. My hunting companion, who had once guided whitetail hunters on the property, told me that the dung-heaps were made by Nilgai, a large exotic antelope native to India. They regularly return to the same spot to defecate.

Archaeologists delight in discovering middens, or heaps of old dung and other refuse. Pack rat middens near Anazasi cliff dwellings have revealed what the Indians (and rats) ate and what the people used for clothing, baskets and tools. Archaeologists who specialize in early American pioneers look for old outhouse sites to excavate. Pioneers not only used them as toilets, they also pitched all sorts of refuse in the pits.....used dishes, broken tools, worn out toys, buttons, and the like. These old outhouses can offer up clues on pioneer diet, and how they lived.

So, turds are not just turds. They tell stories that enrich our knowledge of the critters in the woods. The next time you see me bent over a steaming pile of shivaki, poking it with a stick, be patient. I'm just reading a story.

Bear Shivaki

CHAPTER 13

THUMBS

Have you ever tried bowhunting without using your thumb? Several autumns ago, I arrowed a fat whitetail doe, a perfect dinner deer. After the obligatory twenty minute wait to make sure the deer was down for good, I climbed out of my best tree stand and took up the short trail. I quickly located my deer and soon I was up to my elbows in the deer's warm body cavity. She had expired on a steep rocky hillside and I was working at an awkward angle. I should have simply dragged her to a more work-friendly piece of ground, but I didn't. I am right-handed, but because of the angle, I was using my knife with my left hand and fishing around inside the deer with my right hand.

Predictably, I cut myself. I badly sliced my right thumb. I probably should have visited a doctor and gotten stitches, but, I'm a guy, and testosterone sometimes clouds our brains. For the next few weeks I had my thumb bandaged and couldn't use it at all. It's amazing how much we take our thumbs for granted.

I still had a couple of deer tags in my pack and the rut was picking up steam. I fumbled around for a week or two, trying to hunt without the use of my right thumb. I shoot my bow with my first three fingers pulling the bowstring. I had to adjust my anchor point a bit, with my thumb pointing up like a hitch-hiker, but after some practice, I managed to shoot with a reasonable degree of accuracy.

However, doing the other menial chores that we normally accomplish without much thought proved more challenging....hauling my bow up into the tree with a rope, buckling my safety harness, feeling the edge of my broadhead to verify sharpness, starting my car, zipping up my fly. Without our thumbs, we are no better than possums without tails!

I recently found direct evidence that thumbs have been important in accomplishing wildlife harvest tasks for thousands of years. This spring I was fly fishing one of my favorite Central Kentucky smallmouth streams when I noticed a tractor plowing a tobacco field nearby. I waded out of the creek and climbed the bank and flagged down the farmer. We stood in the brown field, talking about the weather and fishing and squinting into the bright sun until I screwed up enough courage to ask him if he might allow me to follow his tractor for a while and hunt arrowheads in the newly tilled dirt. He muttered something about the price of tobacco versus the price of Indian artifacts, but he smiled and waved me on as he climbed back on his old John Deere.

That afternoon I found bucket-loads of chert, those jagged shards of flint that are sometimes by-products of knapping stone. I did find three intact nice pieces. They were stone cutting tools about three inches long, fairly common in our area. All three had the maker's "signature," a smooth dished-out spot on one side of the tool that is a perfect place for the user to place his or her thumb.

It is easy to imagine a berry-brown Paleo-Indian sitting on the stream bank, making these three tools with the little thumb rests so that as he sliced deer hide or cleaned fish, his thumb would have a smooth, comfortable hold that would increase leverage and minimize fatigue. I can see him tapping on the rock with a broken deer antler, bent over the stone with his bare knees in the dirt, stopping to brush his jet black hair from his face, his hands the color of red cedar wood.

I decided to experiment with these little tools. The first deer I shot this year needed skinning, so I tried out these cutters. Despite being buried in the stony ground for a couple thousand years, they sliced deer meat and membrane nearly as well as honed steel.

The anatomical term for the thumb is "digitus primus." That name may refer to this digit as the first one on the hand, but it may be because it is, functionally, the most important. Our thumbs are not just run-of-the-mill thumbs. They are different from the majority of the thumbs in the animal kingdom because they are opposable. We can extend our thumbs to touch our other fingers, make a fist, grasp a knife, or an arrow, or a flint cutting tool.

Several primates, a South American frog, giant pandas, and opossums all have opposable thumbs. The possum is unique, in that his opposable thumb is on its rear foot. The possum can afford this eccentric trait, because it has a prehensile tail that can grasp tree limbs and convenient objects. But, none of those creatures have the creative brain to tell the thumb complex constructive things to do.

After my deer was skinned, I washed my stone tools and retired them for good. They now reside in a glass case in my office, accompanied by various odds and ends I have collected over the years......an Apache hide scraper, Crow moccasins, Inuit caribou mittens, a couple of Zuni pots, and a Navajo wedding basket. The artistic crafting and use of these utilitarian objects would not have been possible without the human thumb.

The phrase "all thumbs" describes someone who is clumsy and lacks fine motor skills. However, the acts of writing, drawing, and playing a musical instrument, tasks that require the most exact motor skills, would be exceedingly difficult without our thumbs. Whether there is truth in the notion that a higher power created us, or that millions of years of cause and effect and genetic mutation molded us, or whether a higher power created that system of cause and effect, it is clear that by providence, chance, or both, modern man ended up with an appendage that enables our hands to actually implement the ideas of our creative minds. To underestimate the magnificence of this plain little appendage is to ignore the very structure that allows us to do what we do best. So, the next time we shoot an arrow, or skin a deer, play the piano, or grasp the hand of a friend, we should remember that appendage that makes us who we are.

Author's note: This story first appeared in the October-November 2014 issue of **Traditional Bowhunter Magazine**.

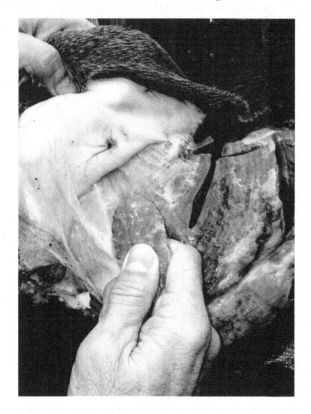

Skinning a deer with the ancient cutter.

CHAPTER 14

THE MCCONNELL HOG

I moved very slowly, taking deliberate steps only when the leaves rustled in the autumn breeze and only when the beast's head was down. For twenty minutes I closed the distance, picking my way around deadfalls and clumps of honeysuckle. I was less than ten yards from the giant hog when I finally took an arrow from my bow quiver and calmed myself for the shot. This did not occur in the swamps of Georgia or the hills of North Carolina. It happened in the middle of a busy urban area.

McConnell Springs is a sixteen acre city park surrounded by retail stores, industrial businesses, and residential neighborhoods. It is less than a mile from the center of downtown Lexington, Kentucky. The property is unique because it is the site of the eighteenth century naming and founding of Lexington and it features several distinctive geological attractions associated with its beautiful limestone springs. It is a small green "wilderness" set amidst the chaos of the urban environment and is used primarily for environmental and historic education. Children's school groups can often be seen walking the trails like their pioneer and Indian predecessors.

That was why the McConnell hog was a problem. In 1999 and 2000 several children glimpsed a pig along the trails and disappearing into the honeysuckle. The pig became one of those urban myths without any substantiation or confirmation. Park visitors would sometimes spot hoof prints in the muddy trails or creek banks, but assumed that an occasional whitetail deer had wondered onto the property.

In 2001, a Parks employee encountered and reported a large pig that did not appear particularly timid. These reports were attributed to the possibility that a hog had escaped from the Lexington stockyards about a half mile away. In September of 2001 I received a phone message from the Parks Natural Areas Manager stating that the hog was back and something had to be done.

At the time I was a Parks Superintendent and I am an avid bowhunter. He went on to tell me that he had contacted the police (who didn't want to discharge a firearm in a city park), the Humane Society (who said if we caught it they would take it) and the Department of Fish and Wildlife ("It's not a wild animal.")

I dropped by the park on my lunch hour and met with a college intern, a nice young fellow who had encountered the hog while doing routine maintenance around the edge of a dense three acre thicket. He explained that the creature was large, black, and somewhat aggressive. It had frightened him with several abbreviated false charges.

I was dressed in a sport coat and tie, but I followed the intern along a paved trail and across a boardwalk spanning a deep bubbling spring called the Blue Hole. We turned and entered the thicket. He led me to the last location where he had spotted the critter. I found a muddy wallow, fresh tracks, droppings, and a large leafy bed that looked like an overgrown bird's nest. The hog had piled up leaves and debris in a large hollow oval, presumably for warmth. We knelt to examine the sign and discuss the situation. I craned my neck back and forth looking for a possible tree stand site. The vegetation was so thick that a ten yard shot would be about the furthest distance I could get from the hog's bed. I bent over and snaked through the underbrush, looking for trails or strategically located trees or anything that might give me an advantage.

Glancing up, I was astonished to see the hog facing me no more than twenty yards away. My companion and I slowly backed away, not wanting to spook the animal from the area. I called the Director of Parks and described the beast. He was very concerned that the creature could harm a park patron, particularly a child. I told him that with a little luck I could find and dispatch the animal to Hog Heaven. We discussed the need for discretion, as this was, after all, a city park with visitors having diverse opinions on conservation issues. He told me I was to avoid swat-team camouflage, no frightening the patrons, no guns, and above all, no wounded hog running around the park. I agreed.

The gate to McConnell Springs is closed and locked at 6 pm, roughly two hours before dark in September. I arrived at 5:30, clad in olive green slacks, a green plaid flannel shirt, and a dark khaki baseball hat, hoping to blend in with the vegetation without alarming any park visitors. I left my bow in the car until the parking lot was empty and the gate was locked.

I shoot a fifty-five pound takedown recurve, heavy cedar arrows, and Zwickey two-blade broadheads. I had harvested several wild hogs, a bear, and numerous whitetail deer with this setup, most of the time achieving a complete pass-through. The Kentucky deer season had just started and I had been practicing every day for two months. I was confident in my tackle and my ability to make a clean shot.

The Parks Natural Areas Manager and the resident naturalist both accompanied me to the Blue Hole, where I whispered that they should wait until I gave them a signal that it was okay to enter the woods. The breeze was in my face as I tiptoed forward. Frankly, I really didn't expect to even see the animal. I figured I would walk around a bit, make a show of giving it the old college try, make a vague plan of coming back if someone else saw the hog, drive home, and watch TV. After ten minutes of oozing forward I spotted what appeared to be the arching top of a buried tractor tire. It was huge, black and motionless.

I stood, focusing on the apparition. With no warning, a huge head appeared, and the hog reached back to lick its flanks. I took a deep breath, waited until the hog lay still again, and continued forward. This is where my story began.

I stopped and took another deep breath, exhaled and drew my bow. I aimed for a tuft of bristly hair right behind the hog's elbow and released the arrow. The hog exploded out of its bed, and I was amazed to see that my arrow had flown exactly where I aimed but I had achieved only about six inches of penetration. The animal streaked into the underbrush and I followed. Twice I lost sight of it. When I finally caught up to it, it was backed up against a gnarly old oak tree, and it was highly agitated. I retreated and circled, trying to come in on the off side, hoping to get an arrow into the other lung. I crept forward and shot once, hitting a branch, missing the animal entirely. My next shot was perfect and the hog collapsed. I nervously backed up and signaled my location to the two park employees.

My original plan, if I actually found and killed the creature, was to drag it out and haul it home, hang it in my cooling tree, and butcher it like I have done with scores of whitetail deer. However, it took all three of us to even roll the critter over. Dragging and lifting it was out of the question. The thing weighed probably three hundred fifty to four hundred pounds. I butchered and boned out the hams and backstraps on the spot. The fat on the hog was four inches thick, explaining the poor arrow penetration. The park naturalist took the head to clean and display the skull and large tusks. We left the rest for the scavengers.

This was not the typical wild hog I had hunted in Florida and Tennessee. It did not have the long snout, lean body, and shaggy coat. Neither was it the typical farm pig I have seen in so many feedlots and livestock trailers. It appeared to be an overgrown pot-bellied pig.

In discussing the events with local wildlife officials, it was speculated that someone may have abandoned the animal in the park, possibly as a pet that had outgrown its home or become too large and aggressive to handle. Maybe it had escaped from the stockyards.

Was there any choice? Experts had been contacted to help and had declined. The hog was clearly capable of harming an innocent park patron, and it had been living in the park for at least two years, becoming less and less afraid of humans. Environmental damage to the sensitive riparian ecosystem was eminent.

I am not proud of this harvest, like I would be of a whitetail deer that I had outfoxed, or an elk that I had tracked high in a wilderness area, animal harvests that normally require wits, patience, endurance or skill with a bow. I was simply able to help with a serious but delicate problem at no cost to taxpayers. While I always enjoy bow hunting and clean harvests, this kill didn't leave me at all thankful, or satisfied or proud or happy, the things I seek in my outdoor pursuits. It left me emotionless.

I read often about people raising animals that go wild...the orphaned lion cub that grows up to kill its master, the tame whitetail buck that gores a farmer, the wolf-cross that kills someone's house cat. Therein lies the lesson. Cute juvenile pets become large adults. We can all do better.

Author's Note: Recent research on wild pigs revealed that in several instances nationwide, pot-bellied pigs that were released into the wild have created human-animal conflicts and were subsequently captured and killed. Wild pig management has become a significant drain on Wildlife agency resources and many states have passed new laws and initiatives to deal with the problem.

The McConnell hog.

CHAPTER 15

OL' BLUE AND THE STONE IN MY SHOE

Why would a sane archer limp around with a rock in his shoe? To add some perspective, I'll take this story on a detour around the barn. I took an anthropology class in college, and learned that many rituals originated out of necessity. For instance, the Jewish rules and rituals surrounding the selection and blessing of food by religious leaders may have had practical as well as religious significance. Prohibition of meats such as pork probably prevented early Jews from infections from meat-borne illnesses such as trichinosis. Early American Indians participated in pre-hunt purification rituals such as using sweat lodges. Not only did these ceremonies help the hunters cleanse their minds and attain focus on the hunt, but they may have eliminated human body odor, much like we use odor-killing sprays and cover scents.

Rituals can inspire. Football players touch a slogan painted on the wall as they leave the locker room to run onto the field. Baseball players have favorite bats. Bernard Malamud, in his classic baseball novel, *The Natural*, compared Roy Hobbs' beloved bat, Wonderboy, to King Arthur's mystical sword, Excalibur. It has been said that Wade Boggs always ate a chicken dinner before each game. The great basketball player, Michael Jordon, reportedly wore his UNC short-shorts under his pro team uniform shorts. Tennis star Serena Williams supposedly wears lucky socks and regularly bounces the ball exactly five times before her first serve.

Bowhunters have rituals. Some have favorite arrows that bring good luck. Some wear lucky hats, like Fred Bear's floppy Borsalino. Our pre-hunt preparations become almost ritualistic and are done in a special order....first spray your boots with scent-killer. Your shooting glove goes in your right front pocket, your grunt call in your left hip pocket...you get the picture. I have an archery practice ritual that I discovered by accident, but now I will not practice shooting my bow without it. It is clearly good luck and has practical applications.

One day last spring I was flinging arrows at a paper deer target pinned to a stack of hay bales behind my house. I was wearing crocs, those soft rubber slip-on shoes you might wear at the beach. I felt an uncomfortable irritation in my right shoe, but took a few shots before I kicked off the shoe and looked. There was a pebble in my shoe, probably from my wife's herb garden. Those shots were badly off the mark, and clearly the result of the distraction caused by the rock. Instinctively shooting my recurve bow requires laser-like focus. Concentration on picking a spot on that animal is absolutely critical, and any distraction that causes me to lose focus may lead to clean misses, and even worse, wounded animals.

Irritations such as the stone in my shoe certainly are not a new concept in our culture. There's an old Hans Christian Andersen Fairy Tale about a pea under a mattress, called the "Princess and the Pea." There's an ancient fable about Androcles removing an irritating thorn from a lion's paw. We've all heard the term "bur under the saddle." Even the Apostle Paul in the Bible had a "thorn in his flesh." The Greek orator, Demosthenes, was born with a speech impediment, so he practiced his speaking with a pebble in his mouth.

Being the brilliant tactician that I am (LOL), I conjured up the notion that if I could train myself to maintain my focus, even while enduring the distraction of the stone in my shoe, I could concentrate on making shots when other real hunting distractions occur.

We have all had to endure mosquitoes while trying to remain motionless before a shot, or keeping an eye on an alert doe or hen when trying to shoot the buck or gobbler. So, I taped that stone in my shoe and practiced with it there all summer.

Fast forward to my Canadian bear hunt last September. I hunted one bear-less bait site for three days before a big wolf showed up under my stand. He had been nosing around my set-up and apparently bears aren't real excited about being around wolves.

Wolf season was still two weeks away, so I was content to watch the critter. Wolves are often vilified as being responsible for declining deer, elk, and moose populations in some areas (and perhaps rightly so) but they are truly emblematic of wilderness. I smiled at my good luck at seeing the beast, and chalked it up as a neat experience. I decided to move to another bait site for the afternoon hunt. The tree I chose for my evening stand was perfect…good distance, good foliage behind me to prevent me from being back-lighted, downwind from the bait, and a perfect height to maximize a double-lung shot.

Thankfully, my outfitter does not use those ugly unnatural bait barrels. He digs a shallow pit into which he places an old truck tire. He puts the bait into the tire's inside "hollow" and covers the set-up with a jumble of heavy logs. The tire and bait are invisible, and the whole thing appears to be a natural-looking deadfall. It takes a bear a few moments to cast the logs aside, giving the archer time to get ready for a shot.

The only problem was a branch hanging down from an adjacent tree between me and the bear's probable position. It did not completely block my shooting lane, but just enough to create a distraction. The limb was way too high for me to reach and trim, so I had to just live with it. The scenario was made worse by a robust breeze blowing the foliage on that limb back and forth across my shooting window.

My stand was in a wooded ravine surrounded by a hillside covered with ripe blueberries. Several times that afternoon I was tempted to climb down and make a stalk on bears I glassed in the distance feeding on blueberries, but I decided to wait it out. The outfitter had gone to a lot of trouble setting up this bait, so I decided to at least give it one afternoon before trying a stalk.

There were lots of blueberries, and I knew stalking opportunities would probably be there the next day. This is a good time to discuss bear baiting. Hunting over bait is admittedly controversial. I have killed a couple of bears over bait, and it is not as easy as some would like to think. I have also tried stalking bears in western states where the terrain and vegetation allow spotting them from a distance, but to date I have not been able to pull off a good stalk. Both methods are a lot of fun and present unique challenges. Baiting is legal in Canada, and is a method necessary for wildlife agencies to achieve the desired harvest numbers and effectively manage growing bear populations. In my book, it is a matter of personal choice, much like hunting mountain lions with dogs or hunting deer over planted food plots.

At around 8:00, a bear waddled down the trail toward my bait. He was a 175 pound boar, not the 400 pounder I really wanted, but it was late in my hunt so I decided to try to kill him. He followed a well-worn trail to the bait and stopped broadside. I picked a spot and shot him perfectly. It wasn't until afterward that I realized that my arrow had probably missed that pesky limb by mere inches and I hadn't even noticed it.

After shooting the bear and waiting until my buddies had finished their evening hunts, we began using flashlights to decipher the clues left by the fleeing bear…a broken twig here and a drop of blood there, matted weeds, and the occasional track in the muck. The trail finally led us to a very dead bear. One of the sweetest sounds a bowhunter can ever hear is someone saying, "There's your bear (or elk or deer.)

I began field dressing the critter while my buddy, Randy, returned to the trailhead to retrieve one of those old military medic stretchers that we would use to haul the bear up and over the rocky trail to the truck. As I was unzipping the body cavity with my folding knife, I nicked the stomach, spilling its contents. I reacted quickly, leaning the bear over to avoid contaminating the meat. Probably three gallons of semi-digested blueberries spilled out onto the ground.

I expected the sour odor of offal, but was amazed at the sweet aroma of warm blueberries, like the smell of Mom's kitchen when she was baking a blueberry pie. No kidding! When Randy returned with the litter, as he now tells the story, my face was inches from the open abdomen and I was deeply inhaling the aroma of blueberries. I had ignored the distracting limb, made the shot, and we humorously named the bear Ol' Blue.

Did my "stone-in-the-shoe" ritual help me kill that bear? Maybe and maybe not. But, that stone is still taped in my shoe. When the snow starts to fly I'll need to peel it out and put it in a warmer boot. I'll definitely continue using that stone's good karma. I wouldn't want to mess with luck.

The stone in my shoe.

Author's Note: A version of this story first appeared in the Fall 2017 issue of **TradArchers' World** magazine.

Photo by Randy Waterhouse.

Ol' Blue

CHAPTER 16

VIDEO

1998 was a strange year. I was still basking in the glory of the previous year's very good whitetail on the wall. I was full of confidence, both in my ability as a hunter, and in my ability to put a razor-tipped cedar arrow where I needed to. Then I was given, GIVEN, an easy shot. And I missed. Yep, I missed.

The white oaks were shedding acorns like rain, and the deer were difficult to pattern. I found a couple of clumps of moist droppings, like raisins, beneath an ancient oak, the kind of tree you might see in movies about mystical wizards. I hung my portable stand in a nearby tulip poplar and settled in for the afternoon. It was only the first week of a three month deer season and I was Robin Hood, or Fred Bear, or Ishi...invincible...the greatest bowhunter who ever lived!

Then he appeared. How he got that close without being seen or heard, I'll never know. This has happened to me before, and I'm always amazed. It's like they appear through a warp in time or space. They're just there. He was carrying a very weird set of antlers. One side was a perfect four point rack, except that it was still in velvet, an oddity for late September. The other antler was a twisted root-of-a-thing, curling down toward the deer's ear. I watched him pawing in the leaves and crunching acorns and I thought of the pros and cons of shooting this particular deer. He appeared fat and healthy, maybe one hundred fifty pounds. His rack, albeit somewhat grotesque, had a certain character.

I considered the attributes of thinning inferior genetics from the herd and I thought of what the landowner, a crusty old cattle farmer, would say ("Shoot the SOB, they're nothin' but garden-robbers and cornfield moochers anyway.") I thought about the promising smell of venison tenderloins simmering in butter. I thought about the upcoming high school wrestling season, and as president of the booster club, how I would be spending more time pushing hot dogs than pulling my recurve. I thought of everything except that I might miss. Perish the thought. And so, when I firmly anchored the arrow at the corner of my mouth, picked a spot low on the buck's chest, and calmly released, I was dumbfounded to see the orange fletching disappear just under the little buck's armpit. He took off like a racehorse, leaving my arrow stuck in the clay and nothing but a memory. That was the first strange event.

Then came the wind. I had never seen it so fickle. Several times I set up downwind of a well-beaten trail, being very careful about the evening thermals, only to have a swirling breeze betray me. I didn't see a deer close enough to shoot for days, and the ones I did see were waving their tales at me like flags as they bounded away. Then my annual pack-in trip to the Daniel Boone National Forest was a bust. My longtime compadre, Tom, couldn't leave town due to prior commitments until Sunday. Like Fred Bear said in his story about the Little Delta, my legs were getting too long for my desk, so I packed up and hiked in on Saturday morning. My plan was to set up camp, scout a little, and get in one or two hunts before Tom arrived. The first afternoon I was hanging a tree stand when I poked a sharp branch in my eye. At first it was merely an irritating inconvenience. But, it got worse and worse until I could no longer see out of my left eye. I climbed down from my stand, walked back to camp, grabbed a quick bite to eat, and hiked the three miles out to my truck. I drove slowly, one-eyed, the fifty miles back to Lexington. I spent the night in the emergency room and the better part of Sunday in bed. On Sunday evening I hiked back to camp with Tom leading me like a blind man, much to my wife's dismay. Monday morning I slept in while Tom hunted.

I finally got up, peeled off the patch, washed the gooey crud from my eye, and went hunting.

Then it began raining. It rained and rained. Despite the soggy conditions I managed to get within ten yards of a nice buck. Or rather, he walked up to me in the post-dusk gloom as I was climbing out of my stand. He snorted and was gone. And that was the sum of my annual backpack hunt.

By mid-November, my eye had completely healed, the acorns had all been consumed, the wind had settled down, and it had stopped raining. I decided to slip out to my favorite whitetail woods on the last day of the rifle season to do a little bowhunting. The afternoon was cool and cloudy with a steady breeze, perfect conditions. High school wrestling season was two weeks away and I knew my weekends were full from here on out. It pretty much was now or never. I hadn't hunted this property for nearly a month. As soon as I left the weedy pasture and walked into the woods, I began seeing rubs and scrapes, lots of them. All right! It was about time! At 3:30 I hung my stand along an old logging road pocked with tracks and lined with peeled saplings. At 3:45 I clacked my rattling antlers together and gave my grunt call a couple of toots. At 4:00 I heard the unmistakable sound of a deer walking toward me in the dry leaves. I turned on the camera.

I didn't mention the camera? I had decided early that summer to carry a video camera during the hunting season. Over the years I've witnessed some pretty amazing things...a bobcat killing a deer, a blue heron catching sunfish, a red fox chasing a grasshopper, a sow bear and three cubs...National Geographic things. So, I started carrying a camera. I filmed a flock of eight big turkey gobblers that afternoon as I drove back to where I normally park in the pasture near the old barn. When I climbed into my tree stand I bungee-corded the camera to a tree limb and pointed it toward the logging road. When I heard the deer walking in the leaves, I reached over my shoulder and turned the camera on. Then I focused my attention on the deer and getting a good shot.

The deer appeared out of the sidehill brush. He was a fat young buck. He walked slowly and steadily, looking for the deer that made the ruckus. At about thirty yards, too far for my recurve, he turned and angled across my field of vision on the far side of the logging road. He crossed an opening at twenty yards and I shot. Just as I released my arrow he stopped and ducked. I shot high and a bit forward and I hit him in the neck. He dropped, spine-shot, like a sack of potatoes. I grabbed another arrow and anchored him for good.

I stood there, fifteen feet above the forest floor, dumbfounded, not believing my luck. I lowered my bow on a rope and started to unbuckle my safety belt. Then I remembered the camera. I bent over to check the on-off switch and I heard the unmistakable whir of the cassette. Could I have actually captured this on film? I decided that dealing with a deer on the ground was more pressing than trying to rewind and look at a soundless image through a tiny aperture while perched in a tree. That could wait until I could relax in front of my TV at home, knowing I had venison on ice.

The buck was no Pope and Young trophy. He was simply a nice representative of the species. His six point rack, while not large, had gleaming white symmetrical tines. He was fat and glossy sleek, like a tan mare. I was particularly pleased, given my weird luck and busy schedule.

This whole episode occurred several years ago, but the buck's antlers still sit on my fireplace mantle, and my young daughter used to chase her friends about the room, holding the antlers on her head, and snorting like a freckle faced bucklet. We ate the venison, some of it smoked, some of it ground up for chili, and some of it marinated in teriyaki, grilled, and served with fresh asparagus and a nice cabernet. I tanned the soft hide and painted an abstract Native American pattern on one side. It's hanging in a friend's fishing cabin.

The venison, the hide, and the horns are trophies, reductions of a living breathing creature to hair and bone and nutritious muscle fiber that are celebrations of the hunt. Normally, reminders of the hunt are antlers on the mantle, the art on the wall, and a memory of the remarkable flavor of grilled venison. However, the camera *was* on, and the deer was captured on film. I can slide the cassette into my VCR and when I hear the delicate footsteps in the leaves, my heart races with anticipation. The buck walks into the picture, there is a streak of the arrow, the crack of bone, and he drops. He thrashes for an instant and another arrow hits him dead center. All is still.

I've watched a truckload of hunting videos over the years, some good, and some bad, and most destined for obsolescence, as VHS technology has gone the way of the buffalo. (And digital technology sure hasn't improved content!) The worst videos usually involve an absurdly long shot and a "hunter" yelping like a banshee afterwards. The better videos usually depict good scenery, a reasonable shot, a clean harvest, and a nervous hunter whispering to avoid spooking a fatally wounded buck. The common thread running through most commercial videos, the good and the bad, is that the camera, usually held by an unseen camera operator, focuses on the animal, moving as it moves, keeping the deer in the center of the frame.

I like my video better. As traditional bowhunters, our role is paradoxical and four dimensional. We do everything humanly possible to place ourselves within the same small grid, at the same elevation and at the same time as our quarry. We go to great lengths to narrow the odds that we will be within twenty yards of a big game animal, that our paths will cross. We attempt to intersect the same grid coordinate and altitude as the whitetail at the same time it will be there. Yet when we do achieve that fateful coincidence of length and breadth and elevation and time, we limit our own effectiveness by choosing a tool nearly as ancient as man himself, a stick and a string.

A video showing the deer walking into, across, and nearly out of that four dimensional space better illustrates the difficulty of our endeavor. Our dreams are frail and when one becomes a reality, so much the better. But, most do not. And yet we continue dreaming and hunting. We are born optimists despite our misses, injuries, fickle winds, and rain. Otherwise, we would stay at home.

So I have my usual trophies. But for this particular hunt, I have another reminder. Sometimes I dust off the old VCR and watch the video, smiling, knowing just how lucky I was.

Video deer

CHAPTER 17

THE OBVIOUS

Sometimes we ignore the obvious and get caught in the old "forest for the trees" trap. As bowhunters, we find ourselves immersed in studying the subtleties of moon phases, various types of rubs and scrapes, and a complex vocabulary of deer sounds. But, there it was, right in front of me, as plain as day.

I knelt in the middle of a small logging road that snaked in and out of the hardwoods on the bluffs overlooking the Kentucky River. The road was bisected by a faint rivulet, no more than a trickle of a stream, crossing a saddle in the ridge. Even though a late September drought had left the ground bone dry, the tiny stream bank was moist and washed bare of leaves. The object of my attention was a set of two large deer tracks, side by side, each going in the opposite directions. I ran my fingers over the tracks. How many hunters had knelt here gazing at the tracks of deer, elk, buffalo, wooly mammoths? Deer tracks are pretty common on this particular property, but these two told a story. They were large, and judging by the moist dirt still collapsing around their edges, fairly fresh. I took the green hay stalk from the corner of my mouth and measured the length of each track. They were exactly the same size.

It didn't take a wildlife biologist to deduce that this old boy had walked both ways on the trail within the last day. I hung my tree stand on the downwind side of the trail and sat down for the afternoon matinee. At five o'clock a flock of turkeys walked by, clucking and scratching leaves in little piles. At five-thirty two nervous does tiptoed across in front of me, just out of range.

At six, I heard the whisper of steps on the forest floor. I leaned forward to see around a clump of sumac and saw antlers slowly turning back and forth like a radar antenna. The buck took a step forward and raised his head, testing the breeze. Satisfied that he was alone, he walked forward down the trail, right at me. He paused at twenty yards and stopped broadside at sixteen. I picked a spot behind his shoulder. At the exact instant I released the string on my little recurve, he took a step forward. My arrow hit him near his back rib. He jumped, hunched his back, and ran over the edge of the ridge. I replayed the shot over in my mind and was terrified. Had I hit him too far back?

After thirty minutes I climbed down and found the back of my arrow in the leaves where he'd been standing when I shot. It was blood covered. I smelled it, expecting the sour odor of fecal matter. It smelled sweet. Thankfully, he had been quartering away and my arrow had apparently angled forward. My normal recovery strategy on an animal that I am confident I've hit well is to proceed in the direction of my last audible contact with the animal, paralleling his exit route, being careful to avoid disturbing the blood trail. If I haven't located the animal within the first few minutes, I circle back to pick up the trail. This time I was lucky. The buck had fallen just beyond where I last saw him.

The arrow had done its job, despite my marginal shot. It had sliced the bottom of the liver, the back of a lung, top of the heart, and front of the far lung. The buck had collapsed perhaps ten seconds after being hit. I walked up and touched the deer with my bow tip. He was dead. I sank to my knees and put my hand on his sleek flank, thankful that my poor shot had resulted in a clean harvest. I stood and stepped back to take in the whole deer. Steam wafted up from his body in the cool evening air. His rack was a perfect five by five with a small additional sticker point on the right side. Eleven points. It was my best whitetail.

I had been chasing whitetails for thirty years with a fair amount of success, and I was still in awe of these elusive creatures. I suppose it is still a residual feeling I acquired during the early days when deer were few and far between in Kentucky, and even sightings were rare. When I walk up to a downed deer, I can still hardly believe what I'm seeing. Normally a specter, a ghost, a promise, here's a deer actually on the ground where I can touch it, caress its smooth muzzle, put my hands around the bases of its antlers. This deer's face was unusually long with a tinge of gray, almost silver, around his eyes. Silver Face. I had seen him before.

One cool evening the previous year, I had settled into a comfortable stand in a tiny grove of oaks surrounded by forty acres of weedy pasture. At six o'clock the farmer cranked up his tractor and started bushhogging the field. He had headlights and I knew he'd mow 'til midnight. I climbed down and hurried to a stand I'd put near a hole in a woodlot fence where trails radiated like spokes on a wagon wheel. At six-thirty two bucks appeared, meandering toward the opening, stopping to occasionally nip at the understory. One was a large bodied six pointer. The other, an eight pointer, had a long silvery-gray face. They ended up almost directly under me on the downwind side of my tree. My scent was drifting, undetected, over their heads. But, the smell of my handprints on the tree trunk was not. I might as well have dropped a lit firecracker on them. One second they were there; the next they had vanished. Late last season I harvested the six pointer. I never saw Silver Face again until now. Both encounters had a common thread. The two bucks had foiled my efforts last year because of the human scent I'd left on the tree. I harvested Silver Face this year because of the tracks he had left in that creek bed.

"We were both betrayed by where we had been," I mused. Metaphors came to mind. Being a good husband, a good father, harvesting a deer well. The deeds we do, the tracks we leave, tell our story. As I looked at Silver Face, drank in his beauty, I wondered if I deserved him.

The game was not fair. Silver Face could not consciously decide where to step, whether to leave tracks in the mud. His reality was only the present, driven by the need to eat, sleep, reproduce, survive. His motives were as pure as the autumn sky. On the other hand, as a hunter, I could have, should have, avoided wiping the perspiration from my face with my gloved hand before touching the lower limbs of that tree last year. And my motivation is the meat, the challenge, pride, fun, ego...sometimes not such pure goals. With clouded motives came an obligation to kill Silver Face well. I had fulfilled the obligation, more from luck than skill. I lifted one of the buck's feet. How can these delicate hooves carry a two hundred pound animal so quickly, so quietly? Perfect engineering. Padded for traction. Pointed for defense and to noiselessly slide under and over and through the leaves. Splayed to distribute weight. Black to absorb the sun's energy on the coldest mornings.

I ran my fingers over the hoof's ebony surface. This marvel of design is what gave you away, my friend. Not the complexities and rituals of your procreation, not the astronomy of the night sky. Just the obvious. A hoof print in the mud. I touched his antler and patted his chest. Stay right here, old boy. I'll be right back. I turned toward my truck to retrieve a lantern and some rope. It was getting dark, and I had work to do.

Silver Face was betrayed by the obvious.

CHAPTER 18

WEIRD DEER

Strange things happen in the woods, and occasionally we get to witness them. Let me tell you about one of the weirdest hunts I have been on.

It was a nice early autumn afternoon, one of those bluebird days we all live for. I wandered around the fifty acre woodlot for an hour or so looking for a likely place to hang a tree stand and ambush a deer. I stumbled upon a clump of three big white oaks and the ground beneath them was covered with acorns and deer droppings that looked like piles of moist raisins. Ah-ha! I had found my spot. I ciphered which way the wind would be blowing as the air cooled just before dark and I went up a straight tall tulip poplar that was growing in front of a big cedar tree. It was a perfect setup to keep me from being back-lit by the sunset.

Just as the sun touched the horizon I noticed movement a hundred yards upwind. I slipped my binoculars out of my daypack and scanned the forest. There he was, a sleek young buck. It had been a very busy year, with lots of work piling up on my desk, and my freezer was nearly empty, so I decided to kill him if he presented a perfect opportunity.

The deer took his time approaching. He slowly walked back and forth, testing the wind and nipping at foliage. He stopped seventy yards out and snorted.

We all know when we are busted. That echoing blow is a sound we dread, as we know a deer has seen, heard, or smelled us, and is warning other deer of the danger.

But I was puzzled. I had been as still as a statue, and I was well camouflaged. I hadn't made any noise, and the wind was in my favor. He blew again, and then three more times. I watched for the tell-tale foot stomp that indicates a deer sees us but is not sure what we are. This deer did not appear to be looking at me at all. He blew again and continued his zig-zag path toward me. Soon he was well within range, but facing me. He began feeding on acorns. I relaxed and dropped my bow limb tip into the nylon holster that hangs from my belt. That little piece of equipment has been taking the weight of the bow off of my bow arm until just the right moment for over thirty years.

The deer worked his way around one of the big oaks and presented another close shot, but he was facing directly away from me and I passed. He blew again and jumped straight up in the air like he had springs on his feet. I shook my head and thought, "What is going on here?"

He took a couple of steps and turned broadside. It was a chip shot, and my arrow hit him high in the chest, angling down through the body cavity. He bounded over the hill, out of sight. I waited the obligatory half hour. I fidgeted, knowing the deer was dead, but making myself be patient. Better safe than sorry. I shimmied down, gathered my gear, and took up the trail. The deer had piled up just out of sight. When I walked up to him, I was elated. What a pretty deer! I rolled him over and stepped back. There was a golf-ball sized black growth on his neck and another smaller black wart below his eye. "What in the world?"

I examined him closely and he looked otherwise healthy. "I sure hope the meat will be OK." I had a couple of nylon game bags in my pack. So, I decided to quarter the deer where he lay. I took a couple of snapshots with my pocket camera and began the process of turning the deer into meat. I lay the hams, shoulders, and backstraps on a log to cool. I then opened him up to remove the heart, tenderloins, and liver. My last chore was to remove the head so I could later boil and bleach the skull.

It would look cool on a bookshelf in my office. I picked up several bags of ice on the way home and put all of the meat in a large cooler and covered it with ice. I put the head in a plastic garbage bag and in a refrigerator I keep in the garage for just that purpose. Right about now, you are probably thinking, "OK. The buck snorted a lot. What is so weird about this story?"

Just wait.

The next morning I touched up my skinning knife with a stone, and fetched the bag from the refrigerator to begin skinning the head. I dumped the head onto a newspaper on the garage floor.

"Whoa!"

The deer's head was covered with maggots. Not those pint-sized ones you normally see on dead critters in the woods. These were gigantic! I'm talking inch and a half long X-files scary big! I quickly kicked the head back in the bag and twisted it shut. I have a buddy who is a wildlife biologist. I called and queried him.

"About those big black warts, did you touch them? " he asked.

"Probably," I said.

"Did you happen to go to the bathroom afterward?"

"Maybe," I said.

"You didn't touch yourself did you?"

"Oh no," I said.

Then he burst out laughing. "Just kidding." he said

"Whew!"

"Those warts are fibromas caused by a virus that cannot be transmitted to humans, and does not affect the deer's meat unless the warts cause a secondary infection. Unless the deer was really sick, the meat will be fine."

"What about those maggots?"

"They are from an insect called a nasal bot fly that lays eggs in a deer's mouth and nose and the maggots hatch in the deer's nasal cavities. The deer then sneezes them out. They don't affect the meat either."

So, the mystery of the snorting deer was solved. The buck wasn't alarmed. He was simply blowing out maggot rockets. My buddy went on to tell me that both of these ailments can infect deer in places where they congregate, like corn piles and deer feeders. I remembered that a hunter on a neighboring farm had a deer feeder.

So, if you ever see a deer that has big black warts and is snorting to beat the band, you'll know what it is. It can be explained, but it is still weird. These days I wear rubber gloves when field dressing and quartering deer. And, yes, I always pee first.

The weird deer, warts and all.

CHAPTER 19

A CAT ON THE RIDGE

Some say a death is a death, that dead is dead. I'm not sure I agree with that. Over the years, warriors have preferred honorable deaths, departures that could be memorialized in legend and song. As bowhunters, we strive for clean harvests, kills that are worthy of our considerable investments in practice, scouting, and equipment, kills that honor the animal. But there are still activists who insist that harvesting game animals is wrong, despite the philosophical, environmental, and nutritional arguments to the contrary. In pondering these questions, I remember an autumn afternoon several years ago.

The early muzzleloading rifle weekend in Kentucky is nearly as popular as the modern rifle season for whitetail deer. Hordes of orange-clad hunters invade the woods. It is no longer a celebration of the pioneer spirit for most, and like many archers who hunt with gizmos that resemble laser-guided rocket launchers, they appear in the woods with in-line rifles bearing telescopic sights. That's perfectly legal, and would be okay I suppose, except that the early muzzle-loading season coincides with the beginning of the whitetail rut. But, then again, my attitude may not be quite fair. We traditional bowhunters can sometimes be snobs.

Hoping to get in a bit of afternoon hunting and hoping to enjoy the great fall scenery, my pal Tom and I drove east into the Daniel Boone National Forest. Every trailhead looked like a Wal-Mart parking lot. We eased our truck between two others at our favorite pull-off and spoke with a hunter sitting on a cooler.

It was lunchtime and he was spooning Vienna sausages from a can with a saltine. We asked him about his luck and how many deer he had seen. The conversation swung around to our stick-bows, that he eyed with some suspicion, and where we planned to hunt. He seemed to think that no one was hunting as far down the creek as we were going because none of his companions wanted to end up "down in there" in the dark. We smiled, waved and wished him luck as we trudged off into the reds and yellows of the Kentucky autumn.

After several hours of prospecting traditionally good deer haunts, I ended up on a high flat ridge above the creek. The ground was churned by deer and turkeys that had scratched for white oak acorns. A well-worn trail meandered up the ridge and merged with another that snaked along the base of a high cliff-line. The two trails intersected in a jumbled field of car-sized boulders that, judging by the size of the trees growing from under them, had fallen from the cliff in the last couple hundred years. There were three good scrapes along the trail in the flat. I hung my portable tree stand on the downwind side of the middle scrape in a tree that would dangle me out over a steep slope down to the creek.

As the afternoon waned and the sun moved behind the mountain, I looked over the ridge behind me and spotted a very good buck, a real whopper. He was making his way along an old logging road that switched back and forth up the slope. I made a mental note of a tree perfectly located so as to give me a great future ambush spot in case the old buck didn't appear on my trail later.

A squirrel barked and chattered up near the boulders and I figured it was scolding a coyote or a hawk. A short time later, I heard a deer walking in the dry leaves on the cliff trail. I'm not sure what made me think it was a small deer. Maybe it was its delicate cadence and the rhythm of its walk. It was probably a yearling or this year's fawn. As the deer entered the jumbled rocks, I heard limbs breaking and the flurry of thrashing in the underbrush. Then the deer started screaming. Screaming.

Several years ago I spine-shot a whitetail doe that immediately dropped in its tracks and screamed. I quickly dispatched her with another arrow, looking around, hoping no one had heard that awful cry. No one dispatched this deer. It screamed on and off for nearly half an hour, each cry becoming weaker and weaker. Finally the deer was quiet. I fished my binoculars from my fanny pack and dialed-in the focus. I finally made out the form of a grey-white furry critter atop the deer. Then I heard the cat. Twice, from over the carcass, it gave a distinctive cry, a drawn out "weough" not unlike the growl we hear on the Kentucky Wildcats basketball commercials. There are no cougars in Kentucky, so I knew it must be a bobcat, and from what I could see, a big one.

The silence and darkness gathered like a blanket. The gloom faded my view in the binoculars. I imagined the cat sitting over the dead deer, one paw casually resting on the deer's long neck, licking the other paw, purring, its yellow eyes peering into the fading light. I quivered my arrow and started my routine of packing gear before descending from a tree. I stopped. Five more minutes, I thought, and settled back in to wait out the last remnants of the twilight. I catalogued to memory the data to later record in my hunting journal, the temperature, moon phase, wind direction, and the big buck on the terrace below.

I thought again of the cat-killed deer. I imagined the deer's wide-eye panic as the cat clung to the creature's neck. Did the deer's limited intelligence allow it to grasp the notion of its impending death? The deer saw the cat, smelled its own blood, felt the claws and fought to live for a half hour. I thought also of the doe I had spined. She never saw me but she obviously knew that her legs wouldn't function, and that frightened her...But for only the few seconds it took for me to nock another cedar arrow and kill her. Which death was more humane? Both deer are dead, one from a razor sharp arrow, and the other from the teeth of a naturally occurring predator. Both were part of the cycle of life. Which was a better death?

The cat will creep away when it hears me climbing out of my tree, only to return and feast for several days. The bones will be left for field mice. The spine-shot deer fed my family, and her soft leather hide is now hanging on the wall. Did the cat kneel over the deer and offer thanks for the bounty of nature? Did the cat reverently open up the deer's belly and watch the steam waft into the cold autumn night like a spirit, or did the cat gently caress the deer's moist nose, asking forgiveness for an arrow poorly shot?

I thought of well-meaning folks who demonstrate and picket the deer hunt at the state park that has had its trees girdled and stripped by starving deer. I thought of disruptions caused by activists at the charity fishing tournament. Can those folks answer the question, can they claim which death is better?

It was dark. I climbed down from my tree, gathered up my gear and met Tom in the valley below. We hiked silently back to the truck, hearing night creatures scurrying away into the blackness of the moon shadows.

Occasionally I have the opportunity to speak with non-hunters about hunting. I think of the cat and the deer and I try to convince them that inserting human hunters into the food chain is not such a bad thing. I hope some of them are listening.

CHAPTER 20

HOME WATER

I've read several stories entitled, "Home Water." I'm sure there's even a book with that name, and maybe even a song. The "Gorge of the Dix" is my name for a three mile stretch of river, my home water. It was the river of my youth and the river that has seen me through births, deaths and other rites of passage. I've never heard anyone else call it the "Gorge of the Dix". In fact, if I did, they would probably be referring to the tailwaters below the Dix Dam.

The Kentucky River cliffs, or palisades as they are called locally, turn upstream from the Kentucky River at the mouth of the Dix River, forming a canyon. Historians say the lower Dix may be the site of one of Daniel Boone's narrow escapes from the Shawnee, the place where he jumped from the cliff rim into the branches of a mighty maple. It is easy to imagine the Indians shaking their heads and muttering something like "crazy white man." According to John Mack Faragher, a Boone historian, another account attributed the death of an Indian who was fishing the Dix to the hand of Daniel Boone. Boone never talked much about it, and perhaps regretted the outcome.

Actually, in Boone's lifetime, there was only one Dix River. It stretched from the southern highlands to the Kentucky River. It wasn't until 1925, that the Dix Dam was constructed, forming Lake Herrington, and thus dividing the Dix into the upper and lower Dix Rivers. The lower Dix River currently is managed as a "trophy" trout stream. If you take a ruler and draw straight lines from Boonesboro to the other pioneer settlements in the area...Fort Harrod (Harrodsburg), Danville, and Logan's Fort (Stanford), the lines all cross the Dix River.

The exact location of the old Wilderness Road is pure speculation, but it undoubtedly crossed the Dix. And of course, it is reasonable to assume that Boone explored all of that territory. The Dix may have been Boone's "home water" as well as mine.

My gorge is above Lake Herrington, where the river runs free and uninterrupted by dams. My normal routine is to park at a bridge on the downstream end of my favorite stretch and wade slowly upstream for six or seven hours, fishing each pool and pocket, stopping occasionally to eat a candy bar, drink water, or maybe to smoke a cigar and just look at the water. The convenience of this stretch of river is that it forms a large horseshoe bend, and a full day of fishing takes you back within a fifteen minute walk of your vehicle. This river is not a big secret. Locals often fish around the bridges, but the complete loop involves bushwhacking through poison ivy and a lot of walking in the rocky river, so it's not crowded. In fact, encountering another angler is rare.

The Gorge of the Dix has great memories for me. I grew up in a small town nearby and could ride my red bicycle there as a kid. I would load it up with my rod, lunch, and a boy scout canteen and pedal five miles to the river on country back roads. Bicycle helmets hadn't been invented, and the roads were crooked. Despite the fact that most traffic would be slowed by tractors and hay wagons, I suppose by all rights I should've been run over. But God watches over kids and fishermen.

The crusty old guy who owned the property across the road from the thicket where I usually ditched my bicycle had built a ramshackle block building where he sold bait from early April until October. Back in those days, the early 1960s, there was a prolific spring run of white bass that was regionally renowned, and it would occasionally be featured in national sporting magazines. Fishermen from all over would show up when the redbuds bloomed to angle for white bass. Most would use spin-cast outfits, like Johnsons or Zebcos, rigged with small bucktail jigs trailed behind bobbers to keep the jigs off of the rocky bottom.

Even at the tender age of twelve I loved to fly fish. My casting skills were learned by watching Curt Gowdy and Bing Crosby and Joe Brooks on the American Sportsman TV show, and reading fishing articles in tattered issues of Field and Stream and Outdoor Life I snitched from the barbershop where I got my hair flat-topped and butch-waxed every two weeks. I had a very cheap fly rod. It cost, as I recall, $16. It was an old bamboo rod and would probably be worth fifty times that today. My favorite white bass fly was a tiny thing called a Lil Skunk, readily available at local gas stations and bait shops in and around Lake Herrington.

One memorable morning found me perched precariously on a mid-stream rock in my cut-off jeans and low-cut Converse tennis shoes, casting my Lil Skunk. After one particularly nice cast into a big eddy, my line jerked and the fight was on. As I recall the event, now over fifty years later, I probably had a six pound leader, and I was terrified that my fish would break the line, so I jumped into the swift water and followed the fish until I could work it into calmer water. I finally dragged it flopping onto a sand bar and pounced on it. It was a huge white bass, around four pounds, quite an accomplishment back in the days before the waters were stocked with hybrids and stripers. I carried the critter up through the woods on a stringer made of a shoelace, and plopped it down on the rickety counter in the bait shop. The owner looked over his glasses, weighed it on a meat scale, and declared me the winner of his annual white bass contest. Looking back, whether there actually was a contest is debatable, but he gave me a prize that is lost in my memory. For two or three years afterward, when the redbuds bloomed and the fishermen from Ohio and Indiana would descend on the river like mayflies, I would ride my bike out there in the dawn gloom and show folks how to catch white bass. The bait shop guy probably charged them around $30 a day for the guide service and he would pay me $10, big money for a twelve year old. But I got to fish and had enough money for more Lil Skunks, and all of the Moon Pies and RC Colas I could devour.

Occasionally a fisherman would tip me a dollar or two, and I eventually bought a cheap pair of canvas hip boots and a Sears wicker creel that made me look like the guys on TV.

One of my big disappointments in life came when I discovered that the Lil Skunk Company had gone out of business, or at least had quit shipping to Central Kentucky. I scraped up enough money from guiding and tips and trapping muskrats in winter to purchase an official Boy Scout Fly Tying Kit. About the only fly I learned to tie was a white and silver marabou jig that was perfect for white bass. I tied it in two sizes and named them the "Big Dix" and the "Little Dix," products of my junior high sense of humor. I still have several in my fly box.

The Gorge of the Dix is beautiful. The cliffs are precipitous, with stunted cedars protruding from crevices. Occasionally I'll see a big redtail hawk floating on the thermals. The gray rocks contrast nicely with the lavender coral-like flowers of the redbuds. The cascading dogwoods on the cliff tops look like waterfalls of cream. The sound of the river rushing over the rocks and shoals reverberates against the cliff faces, like the string of a huge bass guitar. If I'm fishing with someone, which is now rare, I have to use hand signals from time to time, as my voice gets lost in the low roar of the water. In the spring, the water is a dull pewter-like silver. However, as the white bass conclude their spring journeys of procreation, the water turns to a deep green, and its color and temperature are perfect habitat for smallmouth bass. There are dark pools for holing up in the summer doldrums and winter freezes. There are grassy runs that attract fat shiners and crayfish. There are rocky shoals and calm eddies for protection, brushy undercuts, logjams, and shallows, all with varying habitat and food.

I have named the pools and runs after people and events. Buffalo Shoals is where I often see schools of silver buffalo fish congregating and spawning. John's Run is where my brother caught his first fish on a fly rod.

Minnow Rock is where I once saw a skinny farm kid pull bass after bass from a pool using minnows for bait. His cutoff jeans reminded me of my youth. Smallie Run is a deep narrow channel up against the cliff where I can almost always catch a smallmouth high-sticking black wooly buggers like one would fish nymphs for trout. Poison Ivy Pool is only accessible by wading knee-deep through a one-acre patch of poison ivy. I always wear either waders or long trousers there, holding my arms out at shoulder height, attempting to avoid a bout with the itchies. Lunch Rocks is a shelf of bench-like boulders where I seem to always end up around noon. I'll sit and munch a sandwich or strip of jerky while kingfishers wing and chatter up and down the river.

Halfway up the cliff above Smallie Run, on a ledge that is almost inaccessible, there is a small cave. I have never climbed up there. In the summer, the threat of copperheads has prevented me from making the climb, and in the winter, wearing waders would make the climb difficult. I have, though, imagined Boone sitting in the entrance to the cave, warming his weathered hands over a campfire, chewing a piece of buffalo jerky, enjoying the view. Someday I'll climb up there and poke around a bit for arrowheads. A renegade dig, involving screens to sift the dirt for artifacts, would be illegal. Carrying all that gear would be a pain in the ass anyway. Besides, I would rather spend the time fishing, an endeavor for which I am licensed and qualified. I wish I could fish the Dix every day, but sometimes normal life responsibilities keep me away for months at a time. I once found an old Paul Sawyier print in an antique mall. Paul was a late 19th to early 20th century Kentucky watercolorist whose work has a regional following. The print is entitled "The Dix River" and appears to be the spot I call Lunch Rocks. I bought the print and it hangs in my office to give me small doses when I'm away from the river for too long.

Home water is easy to fish. I know what flies to use when and where, and that confidence gives me the freedom to experiment. Sometimes I'll take two rods.

I'll rig one with a streamer like a Clouser or Nearnuff Crayfish, and the other with something totally different, maybe a popper or a cricket imitation. While I'm fishing one rod, I keep the other pointed backward, hanging from my hip in a short slotted section of PVC on my belt. I usually fish the surface flies first. They land softer and don't seem to spook the fish. I'll fish each pocket and run with the surface fly and then switch if no fish hit after a cast or two, prospecting deeper water with the streamers.

The Dix is very fertile water. The headwaters are in the Appalachian foothills to the south, an area we call the Knobs, where they soak through billions of tons of detritus formed by aging hardwood leaf duff, hemlock needles, and sandy, fern-covered slopes. The river meanders down from the highlands and collects the soupy runoff from mom and pop dairy farms, feedlots, and fertilized cornfields. All of this biomass is then cleansed and filtered through natural limestone gravel and a band of karst woodlands that also cools the stream's edges and drops leaves and insects into the clear water. Rich, but diluted enough to minimize summer eutrophication, the stream subsidy ensures that shiners will be fat and crayfish tasty. All of the fish I've ever caught in the Dix were strong-shouldered and healthy.

A few years ago I guided two women friends on a day trip into the Gorge. One had taken a fly fishing class I had taught and the other had never fly fished. It was a warm early summer day and we waded wet. Both of my friends caught fish, and we had a blast pulling eight inch rock bass from potholes in the rocky riffles. It was fun knowing exactly where to instruct them to drop a wooly bugger or Clouser. Like a magician doing a hat trick, it was good for my ego and still makes me giggle.

Despite the fact that cloudy days are best for fishing, I like sunny bluebird days the best. There's a nice big mossy boulder about two-thirds of the way through my typical day that probably dislodged and tumbled from the cliff a million or two years ago.

Sometimes in the spring or fall I lie on the rock and look up at the cliffs and the trees, watching little rock-dwelling birds wheeling and darting after insects against an azure sky. My dermatologist frowns on this unless I glop on gallons of sunscreen. But, the sun feels good on my face.

When I only take one rod, I usually fish with a four-weight, seven and a half foot rig and a six pound test straight leader. Like washing your car causes it to rain, maybe someday I'll hook a seven pound smallmouth because I'm using a six pound leader. Who knows? Of course, a seven pound smallmouth would probably snap a four weight rod in half, but what the heck, it would be fun anyway. Recently, I caught a nine pound carp on a crayfish fly, but luckily my four weight rod was hanging on my hip and I was using an old Orvis six-weight that is as stiff and tough as a two by four.

Home waters have added attractions. The biggest bonus on the Dix is the birds. In the spring I'm usually treated to the distant gobbling of tom turkeys and the screeching of redtail hawks warding me away from their nests. The songbirds are of course the backup singers in this spring chorus. Someday I'll get a book on songbirds so I can identify them by their vocalization. Someone told me that there's even a Smartphone app for that, but now I'm content to just enjoy the music. In the fall I'm treated to big vees of wild geese with their own music. When I was young I read a book called *Swiftwater* by Paul Annixter. I'll never forget his description of the sound of Canadian geese. He described their notes as "elfin." The geese I see over the Dix send their elfin notes down through the clouds, echoing into the canyon. Sometimes I hear the weird fluting of migrating sandhill cranes, but rarely see them as they usually remain above the cloud cover on their long trek south. In early fall I jump wood ducks, the hens flopping around on the water ahead, feigning injury to lure me away from half-grown broods. And then there are the vultures. My Dix River loop has an old dead tree perched at the cliff top that is the perennial roost for flocks of these big black soothsayers.

I like to think of them as nature's solid waste technicians, recycling road-killed deer and cattle drowned upstream in sudden rises in the river. Near the upstream end of the stretch I usually fish, a smaller feeder stream joins the Dix in a rocky, amphitheater-like cove. The feeder stream is called the Hanging Fork. I envision local farmers hanging a horse thief from a gnarly old cedar tree, or from the old bridge that crosses the creek upstream. In the spring, this creek is fishable, but not for white bass, as they would have to navigate around an old mill dam and a waterfall that straddles the stream in the cove. In the pool above the dam, and in the oxygen-rich whitewater below it, I can usually catch fat sunfish and smallmouth. The sunfish have fluorescent-blue spots below their gill covers, much like cutthroat trout have a bright red neck stripe. We call these green-eared sunfish "Chernobyls," musing that their bright colors appear radioactive.

For some reason, the area immediately around the mouth of the Hanging Fork attracts more than its fair share of wildlife. Twice I've seen mink scurrying along the shoreline here. Last year I crept up on raccoon fishing for crawdads, the sound of my clumsy wader-clad footsteps were drowned out by the sound of the waterfall. I reached down and touched him with my rod tip and he bolted like a racehorse into the willows. I've often seen deer on the adjacent hillside, and I usually jump ducks in the big pool below the confluence of the two streams.

One day last year I waded into the big eddy next to the run below the waterfall, casting a muddler minnow into the whitewater. I felt something brush against my leg, and I realized I was completely surrounded by a school of large spawning gar. They finned and moved delicately about the pool, in an almost polite manner, their long bony snouts gently sipping the surface. That is, until I reached down and quickly grabbed one by the tail. The pool exploded in a panicking dazzle of spray as the fish thrashed like a big snake and the others fled downstream. To this day I'm not sure why I did it. I quickly pitched my rod up on the bank and grabbed onto the fish's tail with both hands and held on.

The gar was probably four feet long and had a beak full of razor sharp teeth. I spun in the shallow water, twisting back and forth to prevent the creature from reaching back and biting me. After five minutes of dancing, the fish and I were exhausted. I stood, panting, wet and bent over, holding the fish in the water by the tail. The gar lay still except for the opening and closing of its mouth and gills, its eyes wide with fear and rage. I caught my breath, silently counted one, two, three, and released the fish. I took two quick steps backward as the gar slowly swam in a circle, coming to rest on the bottom, facing me, eyeing me suspiciously. After a few moments, it darted away into the current, leaving a bulging wake. I've done some dumb things in my life. That one was right up near the top of the list.

Once or twice a year I load up my truck and head for exotic trout streams, usually from TU's "100 Best Trout Streams" book: ...Michigan's Au Sable, the Davidson in North Carolina, the Yellow Breeches in Pennsylvania, maybe even a stream or two out west. But, it's always good to come back home to water where one can enjoy a cigar between casts and forget about all of the testosterone-soaked competition with a fishing buddy, or even worse, with one's self. It's nice to lose a twenty inch smallmouth after a savage strike and still smile about it.

I remember standing in the Frying Pan River in Colorado, one of the West's real beauties. The fish were prolific, but so were the fishermen. I stood there, surrounded, not only by the breathtaking redrock canyon, but by an army of other fishermen as well. As the roar of the river filled my ears and the current tugged at my legs, I thought of the cascade of the Hanging Fork at the mouth of the Dix, and I missed the solitude. Imagine fishing in the Rocky Mountains and missing the solitude of a small river in Kentucky, home water. Home waters have the feel of a familiar bed, the smell of mom's kitchen, the sound of a lover's voice.

I'm sure fishermen reading this story wonder why I included the name of the river. This river is not a big secret. Locals fish it regularly, but it is a lot of work. Climbing over slippery rocks, through poison ivy, and a long day wading up- stream tends to weed out a lot of folks. The anglers I know who fish the Dix, like me, always release their catch. If any of you want to fish this river and I catch you with a stringer of fish, you'd better be a good swimmer.

A few years back I fished a small stream in Virginia. On its banks in a shady grove nestled in a patch of wildflowers was a boulder that has been inscribed with a man's name, his birthday and date of his death. I imagined a small group of old fishermen scattering his ashes in the swirling current, toasting his life with bourbon from old tin cups. This was his home water. Maybe someday the same will be done for me.

Fishing the Dix

CHAPTER 21

THE CURIOUS CASE OF THE DISAPPEARING DEER

Hunting, like life, is full of anomalies. If you spend much time in the woods you will see odd things, occurrences that defy explanation, or at the very least make you scratch your head and wonder. For instance, I was doing my annual post-season chores one year...pulling tree stands, helping the landowner pick up trash and mend fences, and delivering barbequed backstraps to his wife, when I made an odd discovery. I had climbed up into a big red oak to remove one of my favorite stands when I found a golfball-sized rock sitting on the canvas seat of the stand. It was one of those geodes, roundish, brown on the outside, with crystals in the middle. I was puzzled. Squirrels have been known to carry around and gnaw on chunks of dried bone for the mineral content, but they don't eat rocks. There were no rocks at all on the ground anywhere nearby, so it must have been carried from elsewhere on the farm. I was so mystified that I climbed the twenty-feet back down and tried a half-dozen times to lob it up and onto the seat, and I couldn't even come close. This particular stand had one of those aluminum climbing poles with steps that fold out. After every hunt, I would unstrap it from the tree trunk and hide it in the brush nearby. When I arrived that day, the pole was still securely hidden and untouched. So, where did that rock come from, and how did it get there?

I once witnessed a young whitetail buck trying to chase a raccoon away from a persimmon tree that was dropping ripe fruit. That deer chased the raccoon in circles around that tree like a scene in a Disney movie. It makes you wonder what happens in the woods when you're not around.

One autumn evening, right before sundown, I arrowed a whitetail doe. I decided to return and blood trail the deer the next morning. When I returned and deciphered the trail, I found that she had expired, fallen against a tree, and was wedged standing up between the tree trunk and a big limb. She was literally dead on her feet. What are the odds? In the fifty or so years that I have been chasing whitetails with a bow, I have had several deer disappear, but with good explanations. "When in doubt, back out" has been my motto when I have been concerned about shot placement, or an initial examination of the blood trail has me worried. On evenings when I know that the cold night air will prevent meat spoilage, I have absolutely no qualms about postponing the tedious job of blood trailing. The problem with this judicious practice is the possibility that predators will find my dead deer before I do. On several occasions I have recovered deer that were missing the rear portion of the hams. For some reason, hungry predators like coyotes prefer to begin their feasts with the rear end of the deer. A couple of years ago I actually had to chase two coyotes off of a buck I had arrowed the previous evening. On one occasion, all I found at the end of a tricky blood trail was a nasty pile of bloody bones and hair.

Luckily, in central Kentucky, there are no grizzly bears, wolves, or mountain lions, critters that will eat your deer and have you for dessert. Occasionally there will be a trail-camera picture or rumor of a black bear in our area, and it is true that they are moving west from their stronghold in eastern Kentucky, but, blackies in the Bluegrass region are as rare as albino bucks. That is why I was so intrigued by the curious case of the disappearing deer.

It was a cool late-November evening. I had seen a few does from my perch along a deer trail on the bluff above the Kentucky River. Despite my sexy bleats and grunts, no bucks had appeared. I was a tad under-dressed and a chill was creeping down my spine, so I was about to call it a day. Just as the sun touched the far ridge to the west I heard a deer walking in the leaves. I eased to a standing position and scanned the forest.

I first saw his tall eight-point rack and thought," Not a monster, but he'll do." The buck paused and walked right down the trail, fifteen yards from my perch. He paused again, I drew, and released. The shot looked and sounded good. The deer jumped and ran. I listened and didn't hear the deer fall, but I knew the shot was lethal. It was getting dark, so I gathered up my gear, climbed down, and took up the trail. I shoot flat, two-blade broadheads. They normally achieve excellent penetration, but sometimes they create only a sparse blood trail. That was the case on this cool autumn evening. I followed the rutted deer trail , searching the leaves with my flashlight for blood. The distinct muddy path ran pretty much directly south until it reached a large deadfall, where it turned ninety degrees to the west. I followed the path past the deadfall until it emerged from the woods at an old broken-down gate. I saw no blood the entire distance. I backtracked to the deadfall, creeping along, hunched over, scanning the ground and surrounding brush for blood that just was not there.

I surveyed the deadfall, wondering if a mortally wounded deer could have snaked through the maze of dead limbs without leaving any sign. With no other obvious options, I put my head down and pushed through the tangle. I emerged on the other side and nearly tripped over my dead deer. He was a mature eight-point buck with a tall, narrow rack. I was satisfied. I grabbed a front leg and dragged the deer to a level opening in the woods nearby. I paused for a few moments, stroked the deer's head, and offered a thanks for its sacrifice and a clean harvest. I then placed my pocket camera on a stump and took a couple of pictures.

It was a pretty good hike back to the nearest place I could park my vehicle, so I decided to quarter the deer where it lay. I hoofed it to my truck and retrieved my pack frame and game bags. Then I began the process of making meat from a harvested deer. I quartered the buck, placing the hams, shoulders, and backstraps on a nearby log to stay cool and clean. I cut off the deer's head, to later remove the skull cap and antlers.

I split open the deer's body and removed the innards, retrieving the heart, liver, and tenderloins.

I sawed off the feet at the knees, loaded everything into game bags and lashed the whole load on my pack frame. I swung the load onto my back, cinched my waste belt and hiked back to my truck.

Driving along the gravel road to the farm gate, I was smiling and replaying the evening's events in my mind like a good movie. As I climbed out of the truck to open the farm gate, I instinctively patted my waist, expecting to feel the familiar bulge of my sheath knife. I stopped. It wasn't there. I stood in the cold night air stomping my feet to stay warm, trying to remember what I did with the knife. Did I put it in my fanny pack before I strapped it to the pack frame? Did I throw it in one of the game bags? I was cold, tired, and hungry, so I mused that surely I didn't leave it in the woods.

I drove home and unloaded my vehicle. I put the meat in a big cooler with two bags of ice and hung up my hunting gear in the garage. My knife was nowhere to be found. I sat on the tailgate and tried to remember the last time I had seen it. I finally remembered setting it on the same log where I had placed the meat. I knew it would be easy to find. The deadfall was a distinctive landmark, the knife was bright orange with an orange sheath., It was right next to the deer's carcass, gut pile, and four feet. The whole scene should stand out like a sore thumb against the dark browns and grays of the forest floor.

I had a business meeting the next morning in a nearby community, and had to drive within a mile of the hunting property on the way to my meeting. So, I figured I would leave early and retrieve my knife on the way to the meeting. Eight o'clock found me back in the woods looking for my knife. I had on a coat and tie, but had slipped on my knee-high rubber hunting boots. I looked pretty silly, but I figured no one would see me anyway. I walked straight in on the game trail to the deadfall.

I circled it to avoid getting my dress clothes dirty, and easily found my knife on the log. Its orange color shown like a beacon. But where was the deer?

The torso, the feet, and the washtub-sized gut pile had vanished. I peered intently at the spot where the deer had been. There was no blood, no hair, nor any intestinal offal. Normally, coyotes will leave hair, blood and digestive matter, and scratch a bare spot in the leaves as they devour their meal. There was absolutely nothing to indicate where the dead deer had been. I looked for drag marks in the leaves. I paced back and forth trying to find a piece of hide or bone. Nothing. What could have carried a roughly sixty pound torso, a gut pile, and four deer legs away without leaving any trace in such a short time? The rational possibilities included a pack of coyotes or maybe a bear. Vultures, raccoons, and possums would leave the bones. Irrational possibilities included Bigfoot, Elvis, aliens, or maybe that black panther that everyone claims ran across the road in front of their car.

The site of the abduction

At the time, I was employed by a non-profit conservation organization and worked with hunters and outdoorsmen on a daily basis. I have told this story to scores of people and no one can offer a plausible explanation. I still occasionally hunt that farm. I have my own place now and hunt it more. But, when I do hunt those bluffs above the Kentucky River, and when I am hiking to and from my stand locations in the dark, I sometimes stop and hold my breath, listening for the footsteps lurking just beyond the glow of my flashlight, the sound of the mysterious creature that made off with my deer. Not really. But I do sometimes wonder.

Author's Note: This story first appeared in the Winter-2016 issue of *TradArchers' World* magazine.

The disappearing deer

CHAPTER 22

WEATHER

Soft snowflakes were floating on the breeze like milkweed down. In the waning light I fished around in my jacket and found my cell phone. I powered it up and wiped the frosty condensation from its screen. I hit the "home" button and whispered to my wife, "Hey...I just shot a deer and need to wait a few minutes. Yep...Good shot. I'll be late getting back." I looked at my watch and gauged when to take up the trail. I knew it would be as easy as reading a large-print book. My cedar arrow had hit the deer in the chest. There should be ample blood on the snow and the tracks would be clear.

The cold was creeping down my spine, so I began some isometrics and forced a shiver to take my mind off of the weather. I thought of the funny saying often attributed to Mark Twain. "If the thermometer had been an inch longer, we'd have frozen to death!" Mark Twain also penned one of the most popular weather clichés in our vernacular. "We all grumble about the weather, but nothing is ever done about it."

There is a growing crowd that actually believes we *can* do something about the weather by decreasing the use of fossil fuels. While I'm all about clean air and water, the skeptic in me questions whether there is a clear link between burning coal, oil, and gas, and weather extremes or even climate change. As I recall from a college geology class, Cincinnati was under a mile of glacier ice as recent as 12,000 years ago, a geologic blink of an eye. Did the methane from buffalo farts and the smoke from Paleo-Indian campfires melt the ice? And what about the Dust Bowl of the 1930's? Our current "record" heat waves pale in comparison to the droughts our parents went through on the Great Plains.

A recent article in the Wall Street Journal (1/12/18), using hard data, pretty much refuted the often used (abused) arguments pushing climate change. And, I'm very skeptical when a messianic guru makes millions of dollars hawking his inconvenient truth like snake oil. We have a saying in here in Kentucky..."If it smells like a pig and oinks, it's probably a pig." But I digress. Let's talk about the weather in less controversial terms.

Back in the 1990's, Central Kentucky boasted a local meteorologist named Brian Collins. He was a great guy who was involved in community affairs and was respected by all. Unfortunately, cancer took him at an early age. Today, two decades later, everyone around here remembers Brian's big miscalculation. He predicted that an upcoming weather front would leave us with a "dusting of snow." The blizzard that night dumped two feet of the white stuff. Years later someone told me the phrase "a dusting of snow" was probably on Brian's tombstone. Brian, ever the comic, would certainly approve. Lesson learned: Weather can fool even the best prognosticators.

Back in 2001, the week before the 911 attack, we were elk hunting at the edge of the Flat Tops Wilderness in Colorado. We woke up one morning to four inches of snow and it was still coming down hard. Concerned that this might be an early beginning to the snow season and that our vehicle might be snowed in until spring, we packed up and cut our trip a few days short. When we emerged from the National Forest near Glenwood Springs, the weather had changed and it was seventy degrees and sunny. We fly fished for a couple of days before driving home. The weather sure fooled us, but it was just as well. We were safe at home with our families when the World Trade Center was hit, changing the world we live in.

This past summer, my buddy John and I were casting flies to hungry smallmouth bass in a local stream. It was a beautiful summer day and we probably caught forty fat bronzebacks.

However, at one point, around lunchtime, a big storm front approached. The wind picked up and we could hear distant thunder as the sky darkened. For the next hour, as the barometric pressure dropped, the fishing completely turned off. We couldn't buy a bite. We finally gave up and had lunch under a big fallen log that was wedged in some rocks. We sat there in the rain, smoked cigars, and told fishing stories until the storm passed. We checked our leaders and knots, gathered up our gear and resumed fishing. The smallies were hungry again and eager to eat our Wooly Buggers and Clousers. I'm not sure why fish are affected by a rainstorm, but they sure are.

I don't care much for bowhunting in the rain. It's difficult to keep my feather fletching dry, despite a weatherproof bag over the tail end of my arrows. And, I always worry about blood trailing wounded deer in the rain. Wet weather encourages me to take up blood trails earlier than I really should. However, one positive thing I have learned is that it is often easy to see where a deer has run in the wet matted leaves. I get down on all fours and peer along the suspected escape route and the leaves that are kicked up create a trail as clear as an interstate highway.

When I was in grad school in Northern Utah, my buddy, Mike, and I decided to go cross country skiing one winter day. We were trekking along a ridge at about 9,000 feet in elevation when a big thunderstorm blew in. Lightning bolts were flashing across the cold sky. As the front approached, it started snowing, Soon we were in a white out. I peered ahead through the swirling snow at my friend and was astounded to see blue sparks dancing on his head and shoulders. I grabbed him and motioned that we should get off of the ridge. We turned and quickly dropped into the timber below. Nestled under a big cliff overhang, we calmed down and poured some hot coffee from a thermos. Mike reported that he saw the same sparks on me. We weren't sure whether the phenomenon was a warning of an impending lightning strike, but we sure were relieved to find shelter from that storm.

Later I did some research and found that we had experienced "St. Elmo's Fire." That was the one and only time I have seen snow in a thunderstorm.

As a Kentucky elk guide, one of my duties is pre-season scouting. Quite often I will leave my home in Lexington at around 3:30 in the morning to be able to be in the mountains glassing for elk by dawn. More than once the factor that has thrown a monkey-wrench into my plan has been the fog. I get up, drink coffee, drive three hours, and have to sit for another two hours on a mountain top waiting for the fog to lift. When the locals encounter fog layered against the mountainsides they say that the "possums are brewing coffee." A little humor goes a long way.

The possums are brewing coffee.

Adverse weather conditions are relative. Warm, clear fall afternoons are good for the hiking, enjoying fall colors, cutting firewood, and bird watching. But that sort of weather can ruin big game hunting. Several years ago I spent a fair amount of time and money on a DIY moose hunt. A week of clear eighty degree days shut down the moose rut and brought out the mosquitoes and black flies with a vengeance. On my last morning in camp I awoke to three inches of snow. Finally! Late that afternoon I spotted a lone bull and began to reel him in with sexy cow moans. He hung up just out of bow range and darkness brought an end to my hunt.

When you get right down to brass tacks, we should realize that most of our hunting is done during transitional periods. They are not quite summer and not quite winter....times when a weather extreme common to either season can rear its ugly head. Here in Kentucky we have a saying, "If you don't like the weather, just wait a minute." Mark Twain couldn't have said it better. I shivered and checked my watch again. I knew it was time to fetch my deer. I stomped the snow from my legs, brushed it from my shoulders, and climbed from my tree. I knew the snow would make sliding the deer out of the woods a piece of cake. I unhooked my bow from its haul rope and turned toward the deer's trail.
The beam of my flashlight reflected off of the snowflakes. I smiled, knowing the chore ahead would keep me warm.

Snow made sliding the deer easier.

Chapter 23

Poor Man's Bonefish

Over a decade ago, I was standing in a stream fishing for spawning white bass. My favorite fly for that species is a small chartreuse and white Clouser Minnow. For some forgotten reason, I switched to a Nearnuff Crayfish., a fly that will fool a variety of fish species. After the third or fourth cast I hooked a fish that was solid and powerful and took me into my backing before I landed it. The culprit was a five pound carp. Wow. I must be on to something. Since that day I have successfully fished for carp using a variety of bugs, from Prince Nymphs to Carp Candy.

One of my favorite spring spawning streams will yield up white bass, hybrid whites, freshwater drum, and carp. I have fun comparing those fish to their salt water counterparts. The whites and hybrids are like ocean stripers. The drum are similar to coastal redfish, and the carp are the poor man's bonefish. If you can catch all three in one day on the water you have what I call the Redneck Slam. However, the carp, pound for pound are the most fun. The most productive method for catching carp on a fly is to watch for circles of very muddy water where the carp are rooting on the bottom like hogs. Strip a fly through that circle of mud and you're apt to get a violent strike.

A few years back, I had one day on the water that defied expectation. It was spring and the streams were high and muddy after a few days of rain. I had scheduled an afternoon off work and I decided to fish anyway, despite high water.

I spent several hours casting various fly patterns that usually worked in the spring...black beadhead wooly buggers, Clousers, Nearnuffs, and even a few nymphs. I came up empty. I was sitting on the bank in a misty rain, trying to keep my cigar lit and contemplating. (Contemplating is something you do when you can't figure out what else to do.) I noticed a pod of carp lazily swimming around nosing the surface of a calm eddy in the river. They were not splashing or slurping like a feeding trout will sometimes do. They were cruising the surface with open mouths, inhaling the debris slick. I scurried down to the water's edge and peered closely at the river. There were little rafts of dead insects that appeared to be some sort of tiny cream-colored moth.

I rummaged through the flies I had brought and I realized that I had left my go-to dry fly box at home. I did, however, find on stray misfiled Pale Morning Dun in my nymph box. I don't remember its size, but I do clearly remember unsuccessfully trying to force the end of a #4 tippet through the eye of its hook. Even after making an angular cut on the tippet with my nippers and spitting on it, the largest tippet I could squeeze through was a #6. Carp are ferocious fighters, so I had a cloud of impending doom hovering over me. I knew if I hooked one it would be a minor miracle to land it.

I tied on and waded into the muddy current. I stood watching the river, muttering to myself something about futility. Finally I spotted a school of carp making my way. I cast the PMD and it landed softly ten feet ahead of the pod. I held my breath as a fish approached and inhaled the fly, and then I held on. It was as tough a tussle as I ever fought. I was trying to keep the fish away from the strong current, rocks, and logs without pressuring the fish into a tippet-snapping run. After a twenty minute fight that seemed like an hour, I netted the fish. It probably weighed around six pounds and was sleek and healthy. I admired the beast and took a few snapshots before releasing it into the current. It was gone like a rocket. For the next hour I caught and released three more until I hooked a fish pushing ten pounds.

It made a run that neither my talent nor my reel's drag could match, and just like that, it broke me off. That little PMD was the only dry fly I had with me, so, I was done.

I returned the next day with a box of dry flies and several spools of fluorocarbon tippet, but no carp were to be found. I finally caught one anemic white bass on a white Deceiver pattern. It didn't fight much. Despite the sunny, pleasant weather, it was one of those "You should have been here yesterday" days. I was glad I fished yesterday.

Poor Man's Bonefish

Chapter 24

The One That Didn't Get Away

This is a true tale. However, I am a fisherman so I am afforded some latitude with the truth. Right on the back of my fishing license it says so. "License to exaggerate." (Not really.) But, this *is* a true story, at least for the most part. All anglers can describe, in great detail, the one that got away. The fish that gets away must be older and much wiser. Otherwise, it wouldn't get away. And of course, getting away adds length, girth, and poundage. It seems fish take a growth spurt after they escape.

Let's see. Where do I start this story? Some years ago, when my daughter was a teenager, she had a good friend who moved from Lexington to Flint, Michigan. My daughter wanted to visit her friend, so I devised a trip that would include her visit and a little jaunt "up-Nort" as Michiganders call it. It would be a great opportunity for me to fish two of the best trout streams in America, the Au Sable and the Manistee, both on Trout Unlimited's list of the "Top 100 trout streams in America." The Au Sable is known as "Holy Water" and upon its banks TU was founded. I theorized that the little town of Grayling which lies between the two rivers, would be a good base camp, a place to prospect for trout, groceries and fishing tackle.

As you no doubt know by now, my two passions are fly fishing and bowhunting. For many years I had been collecting antique fly rods and bows. Grayling is also holy ground for bowhunters. It was the town where the late Fred Bear manufactured bows and arrows from the early 1950's until the 1970's when the Bear Archery Company moved to Florida.

Grayling bows are to Bear Archery enthusiasts what pre-1964 Winchester rifles are to gun collectors. After 1964 and after Grayling, Winchester rifles and Bear bows went to hell in a handbasket. I was thinking that this trip just might shape up to be a dandy. The chances of catching a trophy brown trout in one of the rivers and finding a Grayling Bear lying around in a flea market or antique shop were real possibilities.

We drove to Flint, where we ate barbeque and renewed friendships. I woke up the next morning before daylight to the ticking sounds of an unfamiliar house. I crept around in stocking feet, making coffee in a strange kitchen, trying not to awaken my hosts, excited about the prospects of new water and a new adventure.

It was July 4th weekend, and the interstate running north toward Grayling was like a large river running in a northerly direction, as "up-Nort" is where most folks were headed for the holiday weekend. The flat midwestern farm land began to crease and fold and the smell of tilled earth and livestock gave way to the perfume of evergreen forests.

The first landmark I encountered as I entered Grayling was the Au Sable Fly Shop nestled on the banks of the river. I stood in line behind a family from Ann Arbor renting canoes for the holiday. When it was my turn I asked for a fishing license, advice on campsites, and the best flies to use on the river. The clerk, a youngish college student, smiled and remarked on the "aluminum hatch" of tourist canoes that occurs every day around lunch time. He suggested napping under a shade tree until the predictable wave of canoes subsides. He also advised me to seek out a small out-of-the-way state forest campground, and to use big Hex flies in the morning and small Adams dry flies the rest of the day. I bought a license, a map, a dozen each of Hexes and Adams. I threw my gear in the passenger seat and drove northwest out of town.

I found the campground and it had only one campsite left. I thought, "All right!" The campsite was literally on the Manistee River bank. I knew that at night the sound of the river running over the rocks just outside the tent would be a tonic that no pharmacy could offer. I set up my tent, rigged my rod, and went fishing.

The fly shop clerk had been right. I caught trout after trout on my trusty Adams, but they were small, in the eight to twelve inch range. I fished upstream for several hours until the shadows of the rocks fell across the water like dark sentinels and the cool breeze began to move the tops of the pines. Not wanting to wade back in the dark, I bushwacked through a willow thicket to a gravel road. I walked the mile back to camp, listening to the music of the frogs accompanied by the undercurrent of the river. Halfway back, a pickup truck blinded me with its headlights before I could step off of the road.

Just upstream from the campsite was a small bridge over a feeder creek and a half dozen cars were parked in a weedy pasture. Fishermen were leaning on the bridge, whispering, sipping coffee, pulling on their waders, and stringing up their rods. They were preparing to wade into the black current in anticipation of the nightly Hex hatch. I wasn't interested in wading in a new river in the dark, and besides, it had been a long day and I was tired, hungry, and thirsty. I hung my wet waders on a tree limb next to my tent, and propped my fly rod against a tree. I lit my lantern, and built a fire. Soon a steak was sizzling and I was sprawled out in a lawn chair sipping a beer that was so cold it hurt.

It was a warm night and I slept atop my sleeping bag. Sometime in the night I woke up chilled. I turned on my flashlight and it glowed in the fog that had crept into my tent. I squirmed into my sleeping bag and turned off my light. I fell back to sleep in the dark, imagining I was floating on a cloud.

The next morning I fixed coffee and warmed sweet rolls in a buttered frying pan. I pulled on waders that were still clammy from the river and night mist. I stood up, stomping my boots, wriggling my toes and smelling the spruce fire and the steaming butter.

I fished all morning, catching a few decent browns on the Hex, including one fifteen incher. At around eleven, I pulled out a piece of jerky and a Mountain Dew and sat down on a log. Wings of green algae feathered in the current below the log and a kingfisher sat on a power line cocking his head back and forth, watching me with suspicion . The water was roily, slick and smooth like green ice.

I was reaching into my vest for a cigar when a very large fish swirled in mid-current, directly below the power line. I lit my cigar and watched. There. It sipped another insect from the surface. By the time the cigar was half-burned, the trout had surfaced a dozen times and my hands had started shaking with anticipation. I reckoned the trout was at least twenty-five inches long, maybe even twenty-eight, the fish of a lifetime. I checked the knot on my fly, a palomar that I had tied carefully, spitting on it to grease it before pulling it tight. I was using a brand-new fluorocarbon tapered leader that had been labeled as a 5X, but was probably a bit heavier because I had shortened it by a foot. I was a bit worried about such a light tippet, but I reasoned that there was plenty of room to play the fish if I could hook it. I adjusted the drag on my reel, drowned my cigar with a hiss, and slid off of the log into the current, being careful not to splash and frighten the fish.

I could see that the cast would be tricky because of the power line, so I made a couple of sidearm false casts well downstream for practice. I then slowly waded forward, watching for the fish to swirl to pinpoint its location. The big trout continued to feed, not varying its lie by more than two feet in any direction.

I crept forward and was finally in position. I took a deep breath and exhaled slowly, like I was preparing for a thousand yard shot. I made two false casts and softly dropped the big Hex ten feet upstream from the fish. As the fly drifted overhead, the trout slowly rose upward like a leviathan, but stopped a foot beneath the fly, watching. Then the trout simply sank back down, out of sight.

"Okay," I thought, taking another calming breath. "Let's try again."

I made another good cast. The fly drifted over the fish. Slowly, it came up and casually ate the fly. I set the hook with a short line strip and the water exploded. I felt the fish's weight and it jumped, shaking its head. Then it charged laterally and upstream. The drag on my reel was singing and I palmed it to increase the pressure. After nearly fifty yards of run, the fish turned back toward me. I stripped slack as quickly as possible, letting the line pile up and drift with the current around my legs. As the fish went by me at ten feet, I could see its golden body and red spots and the yellow fly in its jaw. The speed of the downstream run was beyond belief, and I held the line I had stripped between my fingers, hoping the friction I was applying would slow the fish. It seemed to be working, at least for a few moments, but it was all wrong. The line that I had stripped in had drifted downstream behind me. As the trout made its way downstream, that line was being retrieved at alarming speed. And then it hung up on a little downstream bush I hadn't even noticed. I couldn't give the fish any more line. I turned to quickly wade downstream to free my line, holding my rod high over my head, panicking and knowing what was inevitable. Pop. The leader snapped and the fish was gone.

The Hex Fly

I slowly wound up the free line. I waded back to the same log and sat down. I had always heard other fishermen talk about the "one that got away" and I was always skeptical, knowing that fishermen are always forgiven the sin of exaggeration. But now I was the one smitten. And I wouldn't even have to exaggerate. The fish had been a giant. And, frankly, it was entirely my fault that it got away. I hadn't managed my line well and the fish escaped.

"Oh well," I thought, lighting another cigar, my hands still shaking. "Maybe I was hexed by the Hex."

I fished my way back until dusk. That night, between dreams of monster trout, I listened to the rushing of the river over the boulders below camp.

The next morning I was up early. I waded the same stretch of river as the day before, casting silently to upstream pools and eddies, hoping beyond hope to see the fish again, but knowing I wouldn't. At one point I glanced upstream and was puzzled.

A man in a swimsuit was wading toward me with a mask and a snorkel. He took off his mask and slogged over to me to chat. His family had a vacation cabin nearby and he enjoyed swimming in the clear water and watching fish and underwater turtles. He asked me if I'd had any luck. I told him about the one that got away.

"Oh, you mean that big brown under the power line?" he asked casually. "He's still there, lying up under a ledge. Looks like he's sulking. He has a big yellow fly in the corner of his mouth. Biggest trout I've ever seen."

Remembering that all fishermen are prone to exaggerate, and that the heat of battle can warp one's memory, I asked the man, "How big would you estimate that trout is?"

"Thirty, maybe thirty-two inches."

"Oh lordy," I thought. "What have I done?"

I waded back downstream, the current pushing me along like a sail. I stopped at a midstream boulder near camp. I rested my hand on it and said aloud, "Thanks for the music."

I packed up my gear, rolling and stuffing bags and boxes behind the seats and in the bed of the truck. I pulled slowly out of the campground, gravel crunching. I stopped at the bridge and listened to the Manistee for the last time.

I drove southeast through Grayling. As I turned down a store-lined street, I wondered if the folks in the barber shop or the drug store know about, or take for granted, or even care about what they have here.

I drove east out of town and into the countryside. I randomly picked a turnoff and found a bridge over the Au Sable.

I rigged up my rod and pulled on waders that had been drying in the bed of my truck. I climbed down the bank and fished for an hour, relaxing, reflecting. I caught a half dozen trout and I killed the last two for my hostess in Flint. I gutted them at the river's edge and threw them in a cooler with two beers and the last of my ice. I called it a day.

I continued east along the Au Sable, following farm roads along the river. By early afternoon, I drove into the little village of Mio, where I ate meat loaf and mashed potatoes in a family restaurant. My waitress looked like she had pulled a three day shift, but smiled anyway. I left her a nice tip. I was low on ice, so I stopped at a small bait shop in the center of town. It was a typical shop, with a gurgling tank of minnows, and a humming old refrigerator that bore a strip of duct tape with "Worms - 25 for $1" scrawled across it. It had shelves of candy and cigarettes and an old upright cooler for beer.

The holiday weekend had pretty much emptied the store. The shelves were nearly bare. On the wall behind a rack of cockeyed sunglasses and a few dusty Zebco rods hung an old recurve bow. I was immediately interested and I asked the proprietor if I could take a closer look. The man took it down and handed it across the counter with tobacco-stained hands.

It was the most unique bow I had ever seen. It was fairly long, probably sixty-six inches and was made for a left-handed shooter. Its limbs were maple, and backed with cream-colored fiberglass. The limb tips had teardrop-shaped wood reinforcements, and the riser was also maple, but with vertical Osage orange stripes above the arrow shelf. The handle had a gnarled fin-like projection of maple that extended back toward the shooter. Despite being dirty, the bow was quite handsome.

I asked the man if he knew the bow's history. He said that when his father died, they had to move his double-wide trailer from the site, and that the bow was found beneath the trailer wrapped in a tattered blanket.

I ran my hand over the bow's limbs, and asked him if he'd sell it. "Fifty bucks," I stated.

"No way, man."

"Ten-four that," I said.

I paid for my ice and went to my truck. I emptied the ice into my cooler and sat on the tailgate. I thought about the rundown store and the bare shelves. I opened my wallet and calculated how much I had and how much I needed to get home. I walked back into the store and held out a crisp new one hundred dollar bill.

"This is my last offer."

"You'll just turn around and sell it and make money, man."

"No sir." I said, looking him straight in the eyes. "I love old bows and I rarely sell them. I don't collect them to make money. I collect them to....well, for the bows. I'll give'r a good home."

He took a long drag on a cigarette and tapped his lighter on the counter. "Let me call the old lady." he muttered. "Dammit."

The man walked into a back room where I heard something like, "I don't want to sell that sumbitch but my truck needs a new battery."

I could barely make out a woman's voice, but it sounded like, "You're effin crazy not to take his money!"

The man came out and handed me the bow, and I handed him the hundred. I walked back to my truck and wrapped the bow in my sleeping bag and laid it across the back seat.

I drove southeast through small towns with beautiful views of Lake Huron. White gulls floated on the breeze above kids with balloons and families eating ice cream. I eventually turned back to the west toward Flint to pick up my daughter. That afternoon, as I sat in traffic on the interstate watching vacationers trying to go home after the holiday, I could see that they didn't look happy at all. I reached over my seat, pulled back the sleeping bag and touched the curve of the bow. I smiled. This one did not get away.

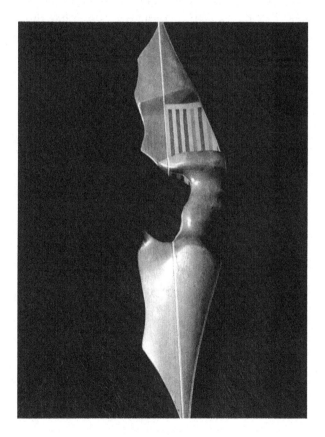

The one that didn't get away

Author's Note: I did stop at numerous flea markets and antique shops on this trip. Not a Bear bow was to be found. I was unaware that one of the reasons Bear Archery left Grayling was an attempt by the UAW to unionize the Bear Archery plant. A strike ensued. Neighbors fought with neighbors and families were split. Bear Archery eventually closed up and moved to Florida. Fred Bear was deeply hurt and never got over his disappointment at having to move from the town he loved and his home on the banks of the Au Sable. I suspect that the dearth of Bear Bows in local shops is related to that dark episode in Grayling's history. Bad feelings die hard. I eventually did a bit of research and discovered that an old bowyer named Ernie Root, a contemporary of Fred Bear, made bows that were characterized by vertical Osage orange stripes above the riser. I suppose it is possible that the bow I bought is some sort of prototype by Ernie Root. But then again, it may have been made by some kid in a high school shop class. It doesn't matter. I like it anyway.

Coming soon! Bill Carman's book, *Hunt Simple,* will instruct the reader on a wide variety of practical alternatives to the pervasive use of electronic and other gadgetry in our hunting culture. The book will be released in the fall of 2018.

Made in the USA
Monee, IL
08 February 2020

21284003R00105